THE WORD

Liturgies, Meditations and Acts of Worship

for Advent, Christmas and Epiphany.

by

Annie K Heathcoat

PIPTIL
Publishing

First published in Great Britain 2018

PipTil Publishing
Glen Garth
Wheatley Rd
Halifax
HX3 5AA

Printed and bound by BookPrinting UK, Peterborough, UK

ISBN: 978-1-9164031-2-3

This book is dedicated, with grateful thanks, to those congregations who have inspired and shared in these services. Thank you for your patience, and for your willingness to join in these new ways of telling the story of Christmas and explore more deeply the meaning of Jesus' birth.

Halifax, October 2018

COPYRIGHT

CONTENTS

CONTENTS 7

FOREWORD 9

ADVENT RESOURCES 11

    Light in Clay Jars – An Advent Liturgy 12

    Light Of God – An Advent Liturgy... 24

    Sing Out God's Praise – A Liturgy based on the Nativity Canticles 33

    Waiting with... - An Advent Liturgy 44

    What Are You Waiting For? – An Advent Carol Service 53

    Your Will Be Done – A Meditative Service for Advent 60

CAROL SERVICES 69

    All You Need For A Perfect Christmas? 71

    Bethlehem.. 81

    Counterbalance.. 91

    Joy To The World 102

    Light Shining in the Darkness 113

    Nativity Canticles 126

    The Hardest Gift.. 136

    With the Poor – A Dalit Candlelight Service................................ 149

CHRISTMASTIDE and EPIPHANY.. 167

    Looking Back, Looking Forwards 169

    Preparing for New Year... 175

    The Lord Has Come! 182

FOREWORD

Initially this collection was going to be called *Christmas Cribs,* playing on the dual meaning of the word 'crib' as a nativity scene, and something that is borrowed from someone else. Then I remembered a letter I had received from a friend when he was working as a Mission Partner in Kenya. He talked about the ways in which the letters "r" and "l" are often transposed in the Kenyan dialect, and the way it made certain Bible passages interesting. He was particularly struck by the verse in the first chapter of John's Gospel which in Kenyan English becomes "The Word was made *fresh*." That seems to be a more appropriate name for these resources which are an attempt to respond to the challenge of presenting a familiar story in new ways, that enable congregations to hear the Good News of Christmas as the incarnation of God. The aptness of the increased when I realised that each of the Carol Services culminates in the reading of the first chapter of John, including the words – "the Word was made flesh and dwells among us".

The majority of resources in *The Word Made Fresh* were not originally written for publication. The carol services have grown out of an attempt to develop some of the themes of Advent and Christmas through the traditional format of a Nine Lessons and Carols service. One or two of them were written to link with some of the Advent liturgies, but it does not necessarily follow that the two need to be used together. Although these services were initially written for specific congregations, they have been adapted for use in a variety of contexts. The adaptations have been to the style of visual aid, the number of readers available and the involvement or otherwise of a choir and/or music group. So these resources can be adapted to suit local circumstances, and suggestions about how adaptations may be made are included at the beginning of each service. The carols suggested are those known by the particular congregation for whom the services were originally written. They can be changed to those known or preferred by the church in which the resources will be used.

Each service can be used in its entirety, with or without adaptations, or the meditations can be taken for use in another context such as private or small group devotion. The exception to this is *Your Will Be Done* as the meditations flow into each other and unite the act of worship.

Most of the carol services use the voices of characters from the birth narratives of the gospels of Matthew and Luke most of whom are mentioned in the Bible, although in some cases artistic licence is used to use the voices of others who are implied. Through their eyes, the meditations attempt to disentangle the meaning of Christmas from cultural and popular traditions that have arisen around the festival, such as the family get-together, or the need to exchange gifts of competing quality. This gives the meditations a certain ambiguity. They can be read at the superficial level of how these characters felt at Jesus' birth or at a deeper level resonate with and challenge the stresses and traditions encounter by contemporary congregations at Christmas.

In each service, whatever adaptations need to be made, the key element is participation by members of the congregation. No acting skill is required, nor is there any need to learn scripts. The main thing is that they reflect on and enter into the spirit of the character in order to bring them to life for the rest of the congregation. Despite the misgivings and reservations of some trained preachers and clergy, congregations have enjoyed working together to respond to the challenge of finding fresh ways to present this familiar story and have found deeper meaning in Christmas through the process.

ADVENT RESOURCES

The Visitation of Gabriel
from the Knitted Bible Exhibition

Light in Clay Jars – An Advent Liturgy

Dalits are the lowest caste in Indian society, often known as "The Untouchables". The caste system is sometimes compared with the English Class system because your caste depends upon the status of your family. However, unlike the English Class system, those born into the lowest caste, the Dalits, find it almost impossible to break free from the prejudice and the slums in which they are confined by law. They have to eat from clay pots as a symbol of their low social stature. They do many of the dirty jobs in society and work in filthy conditions because no one else will do it.

One charity working with Dalits to improve their working and living conditions has started to produce and sell Dalit Candles. These are candles that sit in small clay pots and are all made by Dalits. The candles are a powerful symbol of light and hope coming even to the oppressed, because the lights shine out of the clay pots that are a symbol of their oppression.

These candles suggest an obvious link with the predominant Advent theme of hope, particularly as expressed in the Magnificat and in Jesus' first sermon at Nazareth "I have come to bring good news to the poor, recovery of sight to the blind and freedom for the oppressed." As the Magnificat is used in the Dalit Carol Service, this Advent Liturgy focusses each week on a different part of Jesus' proclamation at Nazareth, often known as The Nazareth Manifesto, to reveal the hope towards which we are working.

The Dalit Candles are available online (www.dalit.co.uk) and from Fair Trade sources such as Traidcraft and the Ethical Superstore. The candles come in a variety of sizes and the pots in a variety of designs that could be used to create an Advent ring with a large central candle for Christmas Day.

The tune for the Advent Carol is Born in the night. *There are two verses to be sung each week, including Christmas Day. The carol is a prayer that God will come and speak and move through us to shine eternal light into the lives of others.*

Pages 20-23 may be photocopied to create an order for congregational use.

First Sunday in Advent - Grace

INTRODUCTION

Today is the first Sunday of Advent. It marks the beginning of the season when we prepare for Christ's coming, not just as a baby in a stable, but also as the King coming in glory and welcoming us into his Kingdom.

Come to your world,
Child of God
to shine your light of grace
Show us your way
Give us hope
And live in us today.

REFLECTION

When he began his ministry, Jesus preached in the synagogue in Nazareth, and said that he was coming to bring the good news to the poor. This means that his Kingdom is one of grace because everyone is included, even those who have no power or influence.

THE CANDLE IS LIT

This advent we are using Dalit candles, made by the Untouchable class of Indian society, to remember Jesus' commitment to those in need, and to celebrate the God who sees light and value in each one of us. Today we light a candle to celebrate his commitment to equality, and our promise to do the same.

PRAYER

Jesus, our King, you come to bring good news to the poor. But these candles, made by the poorest members of Indian society remind us that there is still great inequality in the world, and millions of people scavenge for food on rubbish tips.

Show us how to share what we have what we have with those who have nothing, we pray. For your Kingdom's sake. AMEN

> **Teach us we pray**
> **Child of God**
> **To help the world in need.**
> **Open our hearts**
> **Give us grace**
> **To share the gifts of life.**

Second Sunday in Advent - Trust

INTRODUCTION

We are in the season of Advent.

We are preparing for Christ's coming, not just as a baby in a stable, but also as the King coming in glory welcoming us into his Kingdom.

Today on the second Sunday of Advent we are thinking about God's Kingdom as a place of trust, where those who are held captive by guilt, fear or other people's expectations can find freedom and hope.

> **Come to your world,**
> **Child of God**
> **to shine your light of trust**
> **Show us your way**
> **Give us hope**
> **And live in us today.**

REFLECTION

When he began his ministry, Jesus preached in the synagogue in Nazareth. After saying that he was coming to bring the good news to the poor, he said that he was sent to proclaim freedom to the prisoners. This means that everyone who feels trapped by guilt, debt or loneliness can find the strength to trust that will set them free.

THE CANDLES ARE LIT

This advent we are using Dalit candles, made by the Untouchable class of Indian society, to remember Jesus' commitment to those in need, and to celebrate the God who sees light and value in each one of us. We light the first candle to celebrate Jesus' commitment to equality, and the second to celebrate that Jesus' promises can be trusted, that freedom is possible and to remind us that as his disciples we are committed to being trustworthy for his sake.

PRAYER

Jesus, our Saviour, you promised freedom in God's Kingdom, but these candles made by the poorest members of Indian society, remind us that there are still many people in the world who find it difficult to trust in justice and peace because the political systems are prejudiced against them.

Help us to let go of our prejudice and release those imprisoned by our lack of understanding or forgiveness. For your Kingdom's sake we pray, AMEN.

> **Open our minds**
> **Child of God**
> **To justice and to peace**
> **Challenge our thoughts,**
> **Change our minds**
> **From prejudice to trust.**

Third Sunday in Advent - Truth

INTRODUCTION

We are in the season of Advent.

We are preparing for Christ's coming, not just as a baby in a stable, but also as the King coming in glory welcoming us into his Kingdom.

On this third Sunday in Advent, we remember those who need to hear the truth, and those whose truth needs to be heard.

> **Come to your world,**
> **Child of God**
> **to shine your light of truth**
> **Show us your way**
> **Give us hope**
> **And live in us today.**

REFLECTION

When he began his ministry, Jesus preached in the synagogue in Nazareth. After saying that he was coming to bring the good news to the poor, and proclaiming freedom to the prisoners, Jesus said that he would make the blind see. During his ministry he cured several people of blindness, and they were always the first in the crowd to see the truth about him, that he was the Son of God. Many of us who can see know that at times we deliberately close our eyes to the truth, but Jesus is coming to open them again.

THE CANDLES ARE LIT

This advent we are using Dalit candles, made by the Untouchable class of Indian society, to remember Jesus' commitment to those in need, and

to celebrate the God who sees light and value in each one of us. The first candle celebrates his commitment to equality and the second that he is faithful to his promises. We light the third candle to remember Jesus' commitment to the truth that sets us free and our need to see and hear the truth today.

Jesus, our Healer, you came to bring sight to the blind. But these candles, made by the poorest members of Indian society remind us that there are many people who still want to close their eyes to problems or to deny the truth that all people matter to God.

Help us to open our eyes and minds to your truth, we pray. For your Kingdom's sake. AMEN

> **Teach us your truth**
> **Child of God**
> **The truth that gives us sight**
> **Help us to see**
> **Those in need**
> **And lead them to your light.**

Fourth Sunday in Advent – Love

INTRODUCTION
We are in the season of Advent.
We are preparing for Christ's coming, not just as a baby in a stable,
but also as the King coming in glory welcoming us into his Kingdom.

Today is the fourth Sunday of Advent, Christmas is nearly here and our preparations should be just about finished. But the work of God is never finished, and his love is never-ending. So today we think of the power of God's love that sets free those who are oppressed by fear, worry and doubt.

> **Come to your world,**
> **Child of God**
> **to shine your light of love**
> **Show us your way**
> **Give us hope**
> **And live in us today.**

REFLECTION

When he began his ministry, Jesus preached in the synagogue in Nazareth. After saying that he was coming to bring the good news to the poor, to proclaim freedom to the prisoners and recovery of sight to the blind, he said that he would set free those who are oppressed. This means that everyone who feels overwhelmed by fear or loneliness can hear the words of love that will set them free.

THE CANDLES ARE LIT

This advent we are using Dalit candles, made by the Untouchable class of Indian society, to remember Jesus' commitment to those in need, and to celebrate the God who sees light and value in each one of us. The first candle to celebrates Jesus' commitment to equality, the second that his promises can be trusted and the third that he stands for truth. We light the fourth candle today to celebrate Jesus' love that is strong enough to banish fear, and our promise to share that love for his sake.

PRAYER

Jesus, our Shepherd, you demonstrated God's love to us, but these candles made by the poorest members of Indian society, remind us that there are still many people in the world who feel lonely, who are cast out from their society and are convinced that no one cares for them.

Help us to reach out to the homeless, the lonely, the unloved, we pray. For your Kingdom's sake, AMEN.

> **Reach out, we pray,**
> **Child of God**
> **To those who feel unloved**
> **Help them to hear**
> **Words of love**
> **And set them free from fear.**

Christmas Day - Joy

The four Advent candles are lit before the service begins, leaving the central candle to be lit during the service.

INTRODUCTION

Christmas is here. The waiting is over!
Jesus is born!

> **Here in our world**
> **Christ is born,**
> **alive in hearts and minds.**
> **Showing the way**
> **of God's love**
> **and bringing hope and peace.**

REFLECTION

Today, Christmas Day, we celebrate that God is here with us, sharing in our lives, giving us strength, hope and faith to live in his world.

His final statement in his sermon at Nazareth was that he came to proclaim the year of the Lord's favour. He does this by being among us to sharing our human life and guide us back to God.

 We light the central candle to give thanks for the joy and life Jesus brings.

> **Here in our lives**
> **Child of God**
> **We welcome you with joy**
> **Your light has come**
> **Shining now**
> **And showing us your way.**

PRAYER

> **Teach us we pray**
> **Child of God**
> **To help the world in need.**
> **Open our hearts**
> **Give us grace**
> **To share the gifts of life.**

Second Sunday in Advent - Trust

INTRODUCTION

> **Come to your world,**
> **Child of God**
> **to shine your light of grace**
> **Show us your way**
> **Give us hope**
> **And live in us today.**

REFLECTION

THE CANDLES ARE LIT

PRAYER

> **Open our minds**
> **Child of God**
> **To justice and to peace**
> **Challenge our thoughts,**
> **Change our minds**
> **From prejudice to trust.**

Third Sunday in Advent - Truth

INTRODUCTION

> **Come to your world,**
> **Child of God**
> **to shine your light of grace**
> **Show us your way**
> **Give us hope**
> **And live in us today.**

REFLECTION

THE CANDLES ARE LIT

PRAYER

> **Teach us your truth**
> **Child of God**
> **The truth that gives us sight**
> **Help us to see**
> **Those in need**
> **And lead them to your light.**

Fourth Sunday in Advent – Love

INTRODUCTION

> **Come to your world,**
> **Child of God**
> **to shine your light of grace**
> **Show us your way**
> **Give us hope**
> **And live in us today.**

REFLECTION

THE CANDLES ARE LIT

PRAYER

> **Reach out, we pray,**
> **Child of God**
> **To those who feel unloved**
> **Help them to hear**
> **Words of love**
> **And set them free from fear.**

Christmas Day - Joy

The four Advent candles are lit before the service begins, leaving the central candle to be lit during the service.

INTRODUCTION

> **Here in our world**
> **Christ is born,**
> **alive in hearts and minds.**
> **Showing the way**
> **of God's love**
> **and bringing hope and peace.**

REFLECTION

THE CENTRAL CANDLE IS LIT

> **Here in our lives**
> **Child of God**
> **We welcome you with joy**
> **Your light has come**
> **Shining now**
> **And showing us your way**.

Taken from The Word Made Fresh: Worship Resources for Advent and Christmas ISBN: 978-1-9164031-2-3   © *Annie K Heathcoat 2018*

LIGHT IN CLAY JARS — An Advent Liturgy

Dalits are the lowest caste in Indian society, often known as "The Untouchables". They have to eat from clay pots as a symbol of their low social stature. They do many of the dirty jobs in society and work in filthy conditions because no one else will do it.

One charity working with Dalits to improve their working and living conditions has started to produce and sell Dalit Candles. These are candles that sit in small clay pots and are all made by Dalits. The candles are a powerful symbol of light and hope coming even to the oppressed, because the lights shine out of the clay pots that are a symbol of their oppression.

The tune for the Advent Carol is Born in the night. The carol is a prayer that God will come and speak and move through us to shine eternal light into the lives of others.

First Sunday in Advent - Grace

INTRODUCTION

Come to your world,
Child of God
to shine your light of grace
Show us your way
Give us hope
And live in us today.

Light Of God – An Advent Liturgy

The original version of this liturgy used the petitions beginning "………, Christ comes…" from the Prayers of Intercession for Christmastide in the Methodist Worship Book, © TMCP 1999. For copyright reasons these have been replaced.

Pages 28-31 may be photocopied to create a liturgy for congregational use. The music for the hymn "Light of God" is on page 32.

First Sunday in Advent – Joy

GREETING
God is coming, to interrupt our everyday routine.
God is coming, to reveal his love to those whom others ignore.
Arriving in ordinary, overlooked humanity,
he brings the joy of recognition
by his presence amongst us.

Luke 2: 8-10

THE LIGHTING OF THE CANDLE
Today we light the first candle of the Advent ring remembering the people in this world who think that they do not matter to God or anyone else, praying that God's glorious love will shine into their lives and bring them joy.

Come to us, Joy of the World
Joy for the world we pray.
Show us how to share your joy,
As we walk in your way.

Chorus **O come to us, Light of the World,**
          Shine through in all we do.
          Light of God and Word of Life
          Help us prepare for you.

Second Sunday in Advent - Peace

GREETING
God is coming, to confound our expectations.
God is coming, to challenge those who govern and control.
Demonstrating generosity, understanding and humility,
he brings the peace of acceptance
to our broken world.

Isaiah 9: 2-7

THE LIGHTING OF THE CANDLES
We light the second candle on the Advent Ring remembering those
who are our leaders, praying that God's humble love will shine into
their lives and enable them to bring peace to the world.

**Come to us, Peace of the World,
Peace for the world we pray.
Show us how to share your peace,
As we walk in your way.**

Chorus **O come to us, ….**

Third Sunday in Advent - Hope

GREETING
God is coming, to be welcomed as a familiar friend.
God is coming, to strengthen faithful worshippers.
Fulfilling his promise,
revealing his tenderness,
he ignites the strength of hope in our hearts.

Micah 5: 2-4

THE LIGHTING OF THE CANDLES
We light the third candle on the Advent Ring remembering those people who have spent their lives serving God, often in ways that have not been recognised. We give thanks for the light that has shone from their lives, and the hope they have given to others.

Come to us, Hope of the World,
Hope for the world we pray.
Show us how to share your peace,
As we walk in your way.

Chorus **O come to us, ….**

<u>Fourth Sunday in Advent - Strength</u>

GREETING
God is coming, to share in the struggle of human life.
God is coming, to strengthen us by his care.
Crying with us in our grief,
and kneeling with us in despair,
he enfolds us in his everlasting arms.

Luke 1: 46-55

THE LIGHTING OF THE CANDLES
We light the fourth candle on the Advent ring to remember those people who have remained faithful even when life is difficult, who have prayed for the coming of Christ's Kingdom and the fulfilment of God's purpose for creation. May we have the same strength of faith when we are serving God.

Come to us, Strength of the World,
Strength for the world we pray.
Show us how to share your strength,
As we walk in your way.

Chorus **O come to us, ….**

Christmas Day – Light of the World

GREETING
Jesus is born!
God has come to us!
Revealing his love, compassion and trust,
in the fragility of a baby
and the gentleness of ordinariness.

THE LIGHTING OF THE CANDLES

bringing joy,	_(light first candle)_
peace,	_(light second candle)_
hope	_(light third candle)_
and strength.	_(light fourth candle)_

We light the central candle to celebrate Christ's birth and his presence among us.

As the candle is lit: Christ is born,
the light of love shines in our hearts.
HALLELUJAH!

Christ has come, the light of God
Shines in the world today
Joy and peace and strength and hope
For those who walk God's way.

> **You come to us, Light of the World**
> **To shine through all we do**
> **Light of God and Word of Life**
> **Help us to walk with you.**

First Sunday in Advent – Joy

GREETING

Luke 2: 8-10

THE LIGHTING OF THE CANDLE

**Come to us, Joy of the World
Joy for the world we pray.
Show us how to share your joy,
As we walk in your way.**

Chorus **O come to us, Light of the World,
Shine through in all we do.
Light of God and Word of Life
Help us prepare for you.**

Second Sunday in Advent - Peace

GREETING

Isaiah 9: 2-7

THE LIGHTING OF THE CANDLES

**Come to us, Peace of the World,
Peace for the world we pray.
Show us how to share your peace,
As we walk in your way.**

Chorus **O come to us, Light of the World,
Shine through in all we do.
Light of God and Word of Life
Help us prepare for you.**

Third Sunday in Advent - Hope

GREETING

Micah 5: 2-4

THE LIGHTING OF THE CANDLES

**Come to us, Hope of the World,
Hope for the world we pray.
Show us how to share your peace,
As we walk in your way.**

Chorus **O come to us, Light of the World,
Shine through in all we do.
Light of God and Word of Life
Help us prepare for you.**

Fourth Sunday in Advent - Strength

GREETING

Luke 1: 46-55

THE LIGHTING OF THE CANDLES

**Come to us, Strength of the World,
Strength for the world we pray.
Show us how to share your strength,
As we walk in your way.**

Chorus **O come to us, Light of the World,
Shine through in all we do.
Light of God and Word of Life
Help us prepare for you.**

Christmas Day – Light of the World

GREETING

THE LIGHTING OF THE CANDLES

As the central candle is lit: Christ is born,
the light of love shines in our hearts.
HALLELUJAH!

Christ has come, the light of God
Shines in the world today
Joy and peace and strength and hope
For those who walk God's way.

> **You come to us, Light of the World**
> **To shine through all we do**
> **Light of God and Word of Life**
> **Help us to walk with you.**

Taken from The Word Made Fresh: Worship Resources for Advent and Christmas ISBN: 978-1-9164031-2-3   _© Annie K Heathcoat 2018_

LIGHT OF GOD

An Advent Liturgy

Taken from The Word Made Fresh: Worship Resources for Advent and Christmas ISBN: 978-1-9164031-2-3   © *Annie K Heathcoat 2018*

Light of God

Sing Out God's Praise – An Advent Liturgy based on the Nativity Canticles

This liturgy was written to complement the Nativity Canticles Carol Service. It draws on the themes of the four great Nativity Canticles in Luke's gospel – the Benedictus (the Song of Zechariah); the Magnificat (the Song of Mary); the Gloria (the Song of the Angels); and the Nunc Dimittis (the Song of Simeon). Luke uses these canticles to introduce the major themes of his Gospel – hope, the reversal of the world's standards, the dawning of a new age and the faithful God who keeps his promises.

In this liturgy these themes are drawn out and given an Advent emphasis reminding us that not only are these the agenda of Jesus in Luke's Gospel, but should also be the agenda to which we are working in expectation of the Second Coming.

If the liturgy seems too long, then the reflections that follow each Bible reading can be replaced by a pause for reflection before lighting the candles.

The tune for the Advent hymn is the Sussex Carol. The first verse should be sung each week to introduce the candle ceremony, with the appropriate verse sung to conclude it.

Pages 40-43 may be photocopied to create a liturgy for congregational use.

First Sunday in Advent – Light is Dawning

INTRODUCTION

During Advent we are looking at the hymns of praise that people sang when Jesus was born, what they tell us about his ministry and what that means for our Christian discipleship as we wait for Jesus' Second Coming. Today we will be thinking about the song of Zechariah and the opportunities for new life we receive from God.

We sing a song of praise to God
We sing with joy that Christ is near
We sing to show our faith in God
We sing out loud for all to hear
Sing songs of praise to God all the earth
For the hope God gives in Jesus' birth.

Luke 1: 76-79

BENEDICTUS
This song is known as the Benedictus and it's the song that Zechariah sang when his son, John the Baptist, was born. It's a hymn that praises God for keeping the promises he made to earlier generations. It's a vision of hope, and talks about John as "the prophet of the most High" who comes to say that there is hope, that sins can be forgiven and that God has not forgotten his people. John would be preaching to people who were living in an occupied land, who followed strict religious laws and who often felt that God had abandoned them. But John was coming to reminding them that God keeps his promise, that there is always the chance of new life, we just have to be ready for it. Zechariah describes John as the dawn that leads to the sunrise, the light beginning to shine in the darkness of despair that promises that better times are coming.

THE CANDLE IS LIT:
We light the first candle on the Advent ring to praise God for the gift of new life and hope. We pray that, by the grace of God, we will be able to offer forgiveness and hope to everyone we meet.

John's father sang with joy to God
For his great gift of human life
He sang to praise the faithful God
who has fulfilled His promises.
Light dawns on dark and forlorn dreams
To show God's love and all it means.

Second Sunday in Advent - Hope

INTRODUCTION
During Advent we are looking at the hymns of praise that people sang when Jesus was born, what they tell us about his ministry and what that means for our Christian discipleship as we wait for Jesus' Second Coming. Today we will be thinking about the song of Simeon and the hope that we have in God because he is faithful to his promises.

> **We sing a song of praise to God**
> **We sing with joy that Christ is near**
> **We sing to show our faith in God**
> **We sing out loud for all to hear**
> **Sing songs of praise to God all the earth**
> **For the hope God gives in Jesus' birth.**

Luke 2: 27-32

NUNC DIMITTIS
This is the song of Simeon, an old man who had come faithfully to the temple every day, waiting to see God's promise to him come true. He never stopped believing that he would see the salvation of God before he died, and recognised it in Jesus when Mary and Joseph brought him to the temple. It is very tempting to give up waiting when something doesn't happen quickly. We all have dreams, but it takes commitment and faith to see them through. God gives us the strength to remain committed, if we are prepared to trust in his promises, that salvation will come, and we will see it, just as Simeon did. Sometimes, we just need someone to be with us whilst we wait, to share the tedium and the moments of despair and encourage us to keep going rather giving up and going away. And if we need that, so do others. And we can offer it, in prayer and in person, and show that hope in God is never a waste of time.

We lit the first candle to praise God for the gift of new life,

We light the second for the hope we have because God keeps his promises. We pray that we will always shine the light of that hope from our lives and so give hope to others.

> **And Simeon sang of faithfulness**
> **and God who keeps his promises**
> **He sang of salvation that comes**
> **with divine light of hope and truth**
> **to those who wait in need and pain**
> **God's love will come to hold them again.**

Third Sunday in Advent - Peace

INTRODUCTION

During Advent we are looking at the hymns of praise that people sang when Jesus was born, what they tell us about his ministry and what that means for our Christian discipleship as we wait for Jesus' Second Coming. Today we will be thinking about the Gloria, song of the angels, and the challenge of living in God's peace.

> **We sing a song of praise to God**
> **We sing with joy that Christ is near**
> **We sing to show our faith in God**
> **We sing out loud for all to hear**
> **Sing songs of praise to God all the earth**
> **For the hope God gives in Jesus' birth.**

Luke 2: 13-14

GLORIA

The Gloria is the third of the four nativity songs. It is the shortest and most direct, telling us that God's glory lives in people who live in peace with one another. Maybe we don't find the song of the angels particularly challenging, perhaps because it is so short, or because we are so familiar with it. But God's peace is challenging because it means that we need to forget about our pride and greed, and work together for the good of everyone. Perhaps we have given up praying for peace. We can all agree that the world needs peace but don't know what we can do to help it. Human beings have always fought one another, how can we stop them? Yet, still God promises peace on earth, if we will only listen to the song of the angels, and put God's priorities before our own, and live in peace with those around us.

THE CANDLES ARE LIT:

We lit the first candle to praise God for the gift of new life,

and the second for the hope that he gives.

We light the third candle to praise God for the peace he offers, and pray that we will have the grace and humility to share that peace with God's world.

> **The angels sang of God's peace on earth**
> **A heavenly peace of love and truth**
> **Not driven by love of power and might**
> **but powered by understanding love.**
> **First heard by shepherds alone in the night**
> **We work to share God's peace and light.**

Fourth Sunday in Advent - Revolution

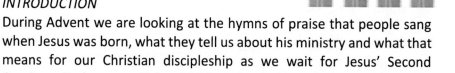

INTRODUCTION

During Advent we are looking at the hymns of praise that people sang when Jesus was born, what they tell us about his ministry and what that means for our Christian discipleship as we wait for Jesus' Second Coming. Today we will be thinking about the Magnificat and God's revolutionary way of doing things.

> **We sing a song of praise to God**
> **We sing with joy that Christ is near**
> **We sing to show our faith in God**

We sing out loud for all to hear
Sing songs of praise to God all the earth
For the hope God gives in Jesus' birth.

Luke 1:46-48; 51-53

MAGNIFICAT

Mary sang the Magnificat when she met Elizabeth shortly after the angel had visited her in Nazareth. She and Elizabeth had a lot in common because they were both expecting children by the power of the Holy Spirit. Mary imagines the way the world could be if everyone recognised the way God works, using ordinary people like her to bring good news and salvation to everyone. She talks of God who throws down rulers from their thrones, feeds the hungry instead of the rich and teaches the proud to be humble. How different would the world look today if people listened to her song, if the proud, and the rich and the powerful could be persuaded to consider everyone's needs instead of their own? But instead of despairing that no one is listening, let us remember Mary's first words of amazement that God thinks that an ordinary person like her is worthy of his trust. God still trusts ordinary people to be the workers of his revolution, to turn the world upside down by upsetting priorities and challenging the proud. And as long as we are still doing that, in however small a way, God's Kingdom is still here on earth.

THE CANDLES ARE LIT:

We lit the first candle to praise God for the gift of new life,

the second for the hope that he gives.

and the third for the peace he offers,

So we light the fourth candle to praise God for the way he can turn lives upside down, and offers new life to everyone, whoever and wherever they are.

We pray that we will have Mary's trust in God and the strength to work for the revolution in human attitudes that will bring in God's Kingdom.

And Mary sang to show her trust
In God's unfailing love for us all
His love will turn the world upside down
The poor and ignored will hear God call
She knew that God will always be just
we sing our praise to God for her trust.

Christmas Day *(The four red candles are lit before the start of worship)*

INTRODUCTION

During Advent we have been looking at the hymns of praise that people sang when Jesus was born that tell us about his future ministry. Today we are celebrating Christmas, that God is here among us again, the fulfilment of the hopes the singers expressed.

We sing a song of praise to God
We sing with joy that Christ is here
We sing to show our faith in God
We sing out loud for all to hear
Sing songs of praise to God all the earth
For the hope God gives in Jesus' birth.

John 1: 1-5

THE CENTRAL CANDLE IS LIT.

The light has come.
The light of new life, of hope, of peace and of trust is living amongst us
And the darkness will never overcome it.

And now we sing that Christ is born
He's born into our hearts again
We sing aloud that God comes near
and walks with us through joy and pain
Sing praise to God in heaven above
Jesus the Lord is born for love.

Luke 2: 27-32

NUNC DIMITTIS

THE CANDLES ARE LIT:

We lit the first candle to praise God for the gift of new life,

We light the second for the hope we have because God keeps his promises. We pray that we will always shine the light of that hope from our lives and so give hope to others.

And Simeon sang of faithfulness
and God who keeps his promises
He sang of salvation that comes
with divine light of hope and truth
to those who wait in need and pain
God's love will come to hold them again.

Third Sunday in Advent - Peace

INTRODUCTION

We sing a song of praise to God
We sing with joy that Christ is near
We sing to show our faith in God
We sing out loud for all to hear
Sing songs of praise to God all the earth
For the hope God gives in Jesus' birth.

Luke 2: 13-14

GLORIA

THE CANDLES ARE LIT:

We lit the first candle to praise God for the gift of new life,

and the second for the hope that he gives.

We light the third candle to praise God for the peace he offers, and pray that we will have the grace and humility to share that peace with God's world.

The angels sang of God's peace on earth
A heavenly peace of love and truth
Not driven by love of power and might
but powered by understanding love.
First heard by shepherds alone in the night
We work to share God's peace and light.

Fourth Sunday in Advent - Revolution

INTRODUCTION

We sing a song of praise to God
We sing with joy that Christ is near
We sing to show our faith in God
We sing out loud for all to hear
Sing songs of praise to God all the earth
For the hope God gives in Jesus' birth.

Luke 1:46-48; 51-53

MAGNIFICAT

THE CANDLES ARE LIT:

We lit the first candle to praise God for the gift of new life,

the second for the hope that he gives.

and the third for the peace he offers,

So we light the fourth candle to praise God for the way he can turn lives upside down, and offers new life to everyone, whoever and wherever they are.

We pray that we will have Mary's trust in God and the strength to work for the revolution in human attitudes that will bring in God's Kingdom.

41

And Mary sang to show her trust
In God's unfailing love for us all
His love will turn the world upside down
The poor and ignored will hear God call
She knew that God will always be just
we sing our praise to God for her trust.

Christmas Day

The four red candles are lit before the start of worship.

INTRODUCTION

We sing a song of praise to God
We sing with joy that Christ is here
We sing to show our faith in God
We sing out loud for all to hear
Sing songs of praise to God all the earth
For the hope God gives in Jesus' birth.

John 1: 1-5

THE CENTRAL CANDLE IS LIT.
The light has come.
The light of new life, of hope, of peace and of trust is living amongst us
And the darkness will never overcome it.

And now we sing that Christ is born
He's born into our hearts again
We sing aloud that God comes near
and walks with us through joy and pain
Sing praise to God in heaven above
Jesus the Lord is born for love.

Taken from The Word Made Fresh: Worship Resources for Advent and
Christmas ISBN: 978-1-9164031-2-3   © *Annie K Heathcoat 2018*

SING OUT GOD'S PRAISE

First Sunday in Advent – Light is Dawning

INTRODUCTION

> **We sing a song of praise to God**
> **We sing with joy that Christ is near**
> **We sing to show our faith in God**
> **We sing out loud for all to hear**
> **Sing songs of praise to God all the earth**
> **For the hope God gives in Jesus' birth.**

Luke 1: 76-79

BENEDICTUS

THE CANDLE IS LIT:

We light the first candle on the Advent ring to praise God for the gift of new life and hope. We pray that, by the grace of God, we will be able to offer forgiveness and hope to everyone we meet.

> **John's father sang with joy to God**
> **For his great gift of human life**
> **He sang to praise the faithful God**
> **who has fulfilled His promises.**
> **Light dawns on dark and forlorn dreams**
> **To show God's love and all it means.**

Second Sunday in Advent - Hope

INTRODUCTION

> **We sing a song of praise to God**
> **We sing with joy that Christ is near**
> **We sing to show our faith in God**
> **We sing out loud for all to hear**
> **Sing songs of praise to God all the earth**
> **For the hope God gives in Jesus' birth.**

Waiting with… - An Advent Liturgy

This liturgy was written for a church who were developing the use of their audio-visual system and wanted to try using a film. They were particularly keen to link Advent hope to contemporary situations. This is why it is presented with suggestions for images to be displayed. Various members of the congregation were asked to record the narration, whilst relevant images were found to accompany script. A recorded instrumental version of the carol was played behind the narration.

However, this does not necessarily need to be done as a film. It could work equally well with the tune of the selected carol played softly on the piano or organ whilst the script is read with the first verse of the carol sung after the advent candle has been lit.

Words in brackets are suggestions for images. Underlined words are the titles for each section and do not need to be read. Likewise text in italics is for display if using an AV presentation and does not need to be read aloud.

 ## <u>Advent 1 Waiting with Courage – O come, O come Immanuel</u>

<u>Introduction</u>   *Waiting with Courage*   (Joseph)

Advent is a time of waiting.

It is not yet Christmas.

Although our minds are full of making sure we are ready to celebrate, it has not yet come.

Sometimes, like Joseph, we are afraid of what lies ahead because we know it will turn our lives upside down.

44

Contemporary Situation   *(Waiting alone)*

During Advent we sing "O come, O come Immanuel, and ransom captive Israel."

Israel had been waiting for a redeemer for many centuries, someone to lead them from oppression to freedom, from darkness to light, and it had taken great courage to remain hopeful when it seemed that God had forgotten and abandoned them.

It can be hard to wait with courage –waiting to hear from family after they have been abroad or waiting for news after medical tests and fearing the worst possible outcome. Sometimes it is hard to even get up in the morning, knowing that we will need courage to simply get through the day.

The good news is that Immanuel means "God with us" – we have courage because we do not wait alone.

Lighting of the Candle   *(A lit candle, or friends waiting together)*

We light the first candle for those who are waiting with courage, afraid of what lies ahead but certain that God will go with them.

Scripture   *(Dawn)*

The word of God came to Jeremiah, son of Hilkiah.
"Because of the Lord's great love
  we are not consumed,
  for his compassions never fail.
  They are new every morning;
  great is God's faithfulness."

Prayer   *(Dawn)*

"O come, thou Day-Spring,
  come and cheer,
  our spirits by thine advent here."

Loving God,
As we wait, give us courage to face our fears, and to stand firm in our faith in Christ. AMEN

Advent 2 Waiting with Patience – Hark the Glad Sound

Introduction   *Waiting with Patience*   *(Wise Men)*
Advent is a time of waiting.
It is not yet Christmas.
Although we may be getting excited about the celebrations
it is not yet time.

Sometimes, like the Wise Men, we have seen the signs and preparations, we are impatient for change, we do not understand why prayers have not been answered and things are not happening more quickly.

Contemporary Situation   *(Christmas Shopping/ Refugees)*
During Advent we sing "Hark the Glad sound the Saviour comes, the Saviour promised long."

The carol talks about long waiting, which requires courage and patience. Western society is unused to waiting – we have email, instant streaming, internet downloads and fast food.

We have largely forgotten what it means to have to wait patiently for someone to be able to help us.

When we do have to wait, for hospital appointments, for someone to come and repair things we need, we get frustrated with delays, and do not understand why nothing is happening. It is hard for us to put ourselves in the place of people who are waiting, patiently, and confused because prayers are not being answered.

The wise men knew that the Jews had been waiting for a Messiah from the family of King David for a thousand years, constantly ready, yet patiently waiting for God's time to be right. They could see the signs that meant he was coming, but had to wait patiently until God gave the sign that he had come among us. Then they could be a part of the welcome and the celebrations.

<u>Lighting of the Candles</u> *(Two lit candles or someone patiently waiting)*
We light the second candle for those who are waiting with patience,
sure that God's time will come, and wondering where they can find the
courage to face what lies ahead but certain that God will go with them.

<u>Scripture</u>   *(Virgin and child)*
The word of God came to Isaiah, son of Amoz:
"The Lord himself will give you a sign:
  A virgin shall conceive and bear a son
  and call him Emmanuel, God with us."

<u>Prayer</u>   *(Healing/ Doctors)*
"He comes the broken heart to bind, the bleeding soul to cure,"

Loving God,
Teach us how to wait with patience.
Open our eyes
to see the needs of others
That whilst we wait,
we can pray for them.
May we never lose the hope that we will see your Kingdom come,
And be ready to serve you whenever you need us. AMEN

 ## *Advent 3   Waiting with Hope – O little town of Bethlehem*

<u>Introduction</u>   *Waiting with Hope*   *(Simeon and Anna)*
Advent is a time of waiting.
It is not yet Christmas.

Although we know that Jesus' birth was the beginning of a new
understanding between heaven and earth,
it has not yet come.

Sometimes, like Simeon and Anna, we have hopes and visions that we
fear may never be realised, and it is hard to keep our hopes alive.

Contemporary Situation *(Bethlehem Wall)*

At Christmas we sing about the little town of Bethlehem, lying peacefully in the night.

But it is a town in the border country which has never been peaceful. It has always been the subject of disputes and war.

Today it is cut off from the rest of Israel by part of the Israeli Wall, which towers over the town and makes it very difficult for the people of Bethlehem to travel to work or to visit friends and family.
It is a place where suspicion and distrust are rife.

And that is the place where God chose to come amongst us, in the midst of human life and hurt.

It was not a safe place then, just as it is not a safe place now, so Jesus' birth there shows us that God is with us, in danger and in safety, in fear and in faith.

Lighting of the Candles *(Three lit candles, or victims of war)*

We light the third candle for those who are desperate for hope, something that will bring an end to suffering and inequality, to violence and war.

Scripture *(Fall of the Berlin Wall?)*

The word of God came to Simeon.
"My own eyes have seen the salvation
 which you have prepared
 in the sight of every people;
 A light to reveal you to the nations
 and the glory of your people Israel."

Prayer *(Baby or light shining in darkness)*

"O Holy Child of Bethlehem,
 descend to us we pray
 Cast out our sin and enter in,
 be born in us today"

As we wait hopefully for your coming, remind us of the reasons for hope in you and your salvation, and give us the strength of faith to share that hope with others. AMEN

 ## Advent 4 Waiting with Faithfulness – In the Bleak Midwinter

Introduction   *Waiting with Faithfulness   (Elizabeth & Mary)*
Advent is a time of waiting.
It is not yet Christmas.
Although we think we're ready and there is nothing left to do,
it has not yet come.

Sometimes we think we know what is coming,
but God surprises us.
So we wait, ready to be faithful in whatever God asks of us.

Sometimes, like Elizabeth, we are impatient for change, we do not understand why prayers have not been answered and things are not happening more quickly, and we have to put our faith in others, and God.

Contemporary Situation   *(Homeless woman and child)*
At Christmas we sing about the bleak midwinter, when frosty winds made moan, and Mary and Joseph took shelter in a stable.

But do we spare a thought for those who have no home, who do not know what it is like to have a place where they are out of the storms? Patiently they wait for other people to make decisions about their lives, where they will live, which language they will speak, where their children will call home.

But like Elizabeth and Mary, they know that God's promises will be fulfilled, that God will answer their questions and come amongst us to surprise and comfort us.

<u>Lighting of the Candles</u>   *(Four lit candles)*
We light the fourth candle for those who are waiting faithfully, sure that
God's time will come, but wondering how much longer they will have to
wait.

<u>Scripture</u>   *(Sunrise or feet walking)*
The word of God came to Zechariah:
"In the tender compassion of our God
  the dawn from on high shall break upon us,
  To shine on those who dwell in darkness and the shadow of death,
  and to guide our feet into the way of peace."

<u>Prayer</u>   *(Offering gifts)*
"Yet what I can I give him,
  Give my heart."

Loving God,
As we wait faithfully for your coming, trusting in your promise that your
Kingdom will come, and justice and peace will walk hand in hand; help
us to see those who are desperate for your Kingdom and are waiting
faithfully for us to remember them, and to reach out to them in your
love. AMEN

   *Christmas Day - The Waiting is Over*

<u>Introduction</u>   *The Waiting is Over*   *(Waiting or people relieved)*
Throughout Advent we have been waiting,
with courage, with patience, with hope, with faithfulness.

[The four red candles are lit]

It is now Christmas.   *(Nativity scene)*
The waiting is over.
So we can celebrate,
celebrate the birth of Jesus and all that it means for us today.

Sometimes, like Mary and Joseph, or like the shepherds, the full wonder of the story doesn't sink in until we have had time to think about it.

Contemporary Situation   *(Angels singing)*

At Christmas we sing about the glorious song of old that came upon a midnight clear when angels bent near to the earth, to touch their harps of gold.

But do we take time to think about what they sang – of peace on earth, reconciliation with one another, the chance to know God's love surrounding and enfolding us? For the birth of Christ is God bending close to earth to embrace it with love and kiss it with peace.

And the carol goes on to say that for two thousand years the angels have sung and pointed the way to Jesus and the love of God, but we do not hear them.

(War zone)

Today, amidst the celebrations, let us stop and hear the angels singing, and pray for peace.

Lighting of the Central Candle   *(A lit white candle)*

We light the central candle to celebrate that the waiting is over, God is with us, Immanuel.

(Angels)

And as we light it, we listen for the song of the angels, reminding us of God's love and desire for peace, and pray for all those who need to hear it.

Scripture   *(Bethlehem)*

The word of God came to Micah:

"But you, O Bethlehem, who are one of the little clans of Judah,
 from you shall come forth for me one who is to rule in Israel.
 And he shall stand and feed his flock in the strength of the LORD
 and they shall live secure, for he shall be the one of peace.

Prayer *(Angels)*

Loving God,

As we celebrate your birth in Bethlehem, help us to listen for the song of the angels, and to allow your love and your light to change our lives. AMEN

What Are You Waiting For? – An Advent Carol Service

The concept of an Advent Carol Service may seem unusual, but it gives space for congregations to think about the ways in which they are preparing for Christmas. It is best held on Advent Sunday as an extra service rather than the main service of the day. It also works well as an ecumenical service because it is non-Eucharistic.

The theme of this service is "What are you waiting for?" which encompasses not just the wait for Christmas but is also a challenge to think whether we are waiting passively or actively for the coming of the Kingdom.

Some of the carols listed here may be unfamiliar. The first time this service was used coincided with the publication of Singing the Faith, *(Methodist Publishing, 2011) which created an opportunity to explore some of the new Advent material that had been included. Where these carols are not easily available, it should be possible to substitute others which pick up the theme.*

This service works well if there is the facility to project images onto a screen as they prompt reflection on the issues raised. Images relevant to each topic/meditation can be found on the internet, but copyright needs to be acknowledged if these are used.

Whether or not images are used, there should be a pause for individual prayer and reflection after each section. An appropriate chant such as "Maranatha" from the Taizé community could be sung or played during this time.

WHAT ARE YOU WAITING FOR?

Call to Worship – Lamentations 3:25-26

CAROL – O COME, O COME IMMANUEL

(If appropriate an Advent Liturgy may be used here)

Opening Prayers
Into the busyness of preparation,
come, Lord, with your stillness;
Come, Living God, come.

Into the excitement of celebration,
come, Lord, with your peace;
Come, Living God, come.

Into the stillness and quiet,
come, Lord, with your light;
Come, Living God, come.

Come, Living God
and open our hearts and minds
to hear your word
and prepare for your coming Kingdom.
AMEN

The Israelites waited for thousands of years for the promised Messiah. They waited, patiently and impatiently, actively and quietly, with questions and in silence, always sure that a Messiah would come, but never quite sure what the Messiah would bring.

Do we know what we are waiting for and praying for?

CAROL – JESUS IS THE HEART OF CHRISTMAS

Luke 1: 67-79 or the Benedictus said antiphonally

Waiting for God
We wait for God
crying out
or silently,
patiently
or impatiently.

We wait,
trusting in his promise
to be with us always,
we wait
because there is nothing else we can do.
we wait
because he has promised he will come again,
and that gives us hope,
that dawns in our hearts
and wakens us to new life.

Silence, or chant

Lord, we are in a time of waiting.
We are impatient
We want answers
We want results
and we want them now.

Come
into our waiting time,
into our impatience
and teach us your way
of listening and praying.
Come, Living God, come.

CAROL – INTO THE DARKNESS OF THIS WORLD

Isaiah 40: 1-5

What are we waiting for?
Do we know what we are waiting for, longing for, hoping for?

Are we waiting for change, a change about which we can do nothing, except wait, like slaves going to market, ready to be bought and sold, wondering with trepidation what will happen to us?

Or are we waiting for opportunities, for education, for freedom from responsibilities, for release from oppression, for time to explore our skills?

Or are we waiting with everyone else, because we all want to go in the same direction, like travellers at a bus stop, united by the need to travel, by having the same destination, or because we don't want to be left behind?

Silence or chant

Lord, we are in a time of expectation
We are hopeful
We are excited
We are fearful
of other's expectations of us.

Come,
To our waiting hearts,
to your waiting world
and show us your light.
Come, Living God, come.

CAROL – PRAISE TO THE GOD WHO CLEARS THE WAY

1 Corinthians 1: 3-9

How do we wait?
How are we waiting for God?

Are we excitedly counting down the days like a child waiting for a treat, anticipating the joy that it will bring?

56

Are we uncertain, like those waiting for the results of medical tests or treatment, wondering what the outcome will be?

Are we prayerful, listening for God, discerning God's will, asking for strength and fulfilment?

Or are we busy, rushing around, trying to make everything perfect, so that when the time comes we are too exhausted to enjoy it?

Or are we waiting with longing, like a child or a faithful pet, waiting for the beloved friend to return, waiting, until he comes?

Silence or chant

Lord, we are in a time of preparing
We are busy
We are distracted
We have no time to listen.

Come,
into our busyness
into our distraction
into our determination to get it right
and teach us to look for your Kingdom.
Come, Living God, come.

CAROL – COME, THOU LONG-EXPECTED JESUS

Why do we wait?
Towards the end of the book of Isaiah, the prophet turns to God in despair and says "O that you would rend the heavens and come down". It's something we may all feel at some time, looking at the world around us. "Why don't you do something God?"

And we wait for an answer, wondering if God is listening. At times the world taunts us, suggesting we shouldn't wait, that it's a waste of time. Yet, we carry on waiting for God's time to be right.

Because we know that God keeps the promises he makes. God has rent the heavens, he has fulfilled his promise, "In the tender compassion of our God, the dawn from on high has come"

To those waiting with trepidation, we offer the words of the psalmist – "The Lord is my light and my salvation, whom then shall I fear?"

To those waiting for opportunities, for an end to racism, poverty, and inequality, we offer the words of Jesus "I have come that you might have life, and have it in all its fullness".

To those travelling the same road, towards the same destination, waiting with us, we offer a hand of friendship.

To those waiting with uncertainty to presence, we come alongside and offer them the hand of God and the words of Isaiah "Do not be afraid, I am with you."

We find that as we wait, God is answering prayer in us, and that waiting is not passive, but active. And we know that our prayers are answered – that through the tireless campaigning of those who were not prepared to sit and wait, we now live in world where there is more equality and much less slavery.

We live in a world where opportunities are created by aid programmes, and by people prepared to work with those scorned by others.

We can be the Kingdom of God, whilst we wait for Christ to come again, waiting for Christ, as Christ's body.

For we do this to proclaim the new life, new hope, and the Kingdom of God in whom we believe, until he comes.

So what are you waiting for now?

CAROL – INTO THE DARKNESS OF THIS WORLD

Prayers of Intercession
Loving God,
As we wait for your coming,
we place into your hands
those who are waiting:

> for an end to suffering,
>
> for a ceasefire in a never-ending war,
>
> for understanding,
>
> for hope,
>
> for friendship,
>
> for healing.

Silence or chant

Come, Lord Jesus,
Hear our cries
Answer our prayers
Comes into our questions of despair
with answers of hope.
Come, Living God, come. AMEN

The Lord's Prayer

CAROL - HARK THE GLAD SOUND THE SAVIOUR COMES

Blessing
God be with us in our waiting,
in our preparations, and our excitement,
our anticipation and our action,
and may his blessing remain on us all, now and always. **AMEN**

Your Will Be Done – A Meditative Service for Advent

This meditation was originally written under the pen name of Kathryn White. It was commissioned by Magnet, a magazine that was part of the work of the Women's Network of the Methodist Church. It is a continuous meditation interspersed with hymns and prayers so that can be used as a complete act of worship. It is designed for use particularly in women's meetings and is written from the point of view of Mary's mother to reflect some of the experiences of mothers and grandmothers in contemporary society.

The service can be read by one person or shared between several.

For each section, visual aids are suggested which, together with a cross, make the link between the Incarnation and the Passion of Christ. Arrange the objects in a circle on a centrally placed table, adding the cross to the middle of the circle during the closing prayers. As the prayer which ends each section is spoken, you may like to light a candle and place it beside the appropriate visual aid.

Suggestions are made for appropriate hymns, but these can be changed so that they are more appropriate to the congregation or season.

YOUR WILL BE DONE

Call to Worship:
Come, hear the good news,
God's kingdom is coming,
is coming to all.

Hymn **COME, THOU LONG-EXPECTED JESUS**
      or **IN THE BLEAK MID-WINTER**

Reading: Luke 1:26-35

Visual aid — hammer and nails

My daughter's engaged to a carpenter.
He's a nice enough man,
got a good trade,
and seems to be respectable.
Or so I thought.

Last night she told us that she's pregnant.
I know that I should be dancing with joy,
a grandchild, my first grandchild.
But she is not married,
only engaged, to this carpenter.
Why couldn't she wait?
We had to in my day.
I do not know what to say to her.
Do I congratulate or condemn?
Her father has found this so hard to take.
She came bursting in to tell us,
eyes alight with sheer joy.
And suddenly he shrank into himself,
she was no longer his perfect daughter,
he no longer had her whole heart.
He stared at his feet,
unable to meet her shining eyes,
able only to mutter into his beard
and shuffle awkwardly out of the room.

Pause

She tells me that this is a special child,
that this child will save the world,
will be the one to right the wrongs of all generations.

How can I tell her
that all women feel this about their child,
that the child in the womb has the greatest potential
and will be the best, most gifted person
and will be able to do no wrong?
She tells me an angel visited her,
and I tell her that I do not want to know.
God does not bother with ordinary peasants, like us.
But she is young, and full of ideas.
How soon that will change when the baby comes!

A candle may be lit.

O Lord, help me.
I don't understand what's happening,
and I feel let down by someone I love.
I am so confused and don't know where to turn.
Give me strength and wisdom to face the coming days. AMEN

Hymn - **THE ANGEL GABRIEL FROM HEAVEN CAME**

Reading: Matthew 1:18-24

Visual aid — A pile of money

I've sent her away.
Paid out hard-earned money
to hide her shame, and mine.
Is this what betrayal feels like?
She's gone to visit her cousin.
Well, the gossips got hold of her.
It didn't take long for them to work it out,
the sickness, and the crying,
the cravings for food.
Her betrothed wasn't too sympathetic either.
He came round for a private talk with her father.

I had heard a rumour he was thinking of leaving her,
walking away from the disgrace,
leaving her holding the baby
and denying that it was his.
But he came to make arrangements for the wedding,
and to deny the rumours.
He said something about an angel too.
What is it with the younger generation,
why do they blame God,
instead of taking responsibility themselves?

Pause

I hope my girl's all right.
I didn't really want to send her away,
but it was for the best really.
And maybe her cousin will talk sense to her.
'It was unkind, possibly,
to send a girl expecting a baby
to stay with a middle-aged woman
who is childless.
But they have always got on well,
and she couldn't take any more gossip
and pointing fingers.
No one believes her stories of angels
and sons of God.

A candle may be lit.

Dear Lord, forgive me for gossiping,
for my love of knowing everyone else's business
and sharing it with others.
Help those whose lives are made a misery by false rumours
and by people jumping to the wrong conclusion.
Make me more tolerant,
and more ready to accept someone else's troubles

without sharing them with everyone I meet. AMEN

Hymn – **TELL OUT MY SOUL, THE GREATNESS OF THE LORD**

Reading: Luke 1:39-45; 56

Visual aid — cup and plate

We welcomed her home with a feast.
It was the least we could do.
She was tired after the journey,
but she was pleased with the fuss.
Her brothers and sisters spent hours preparing,
baking bread, cleaning the room.

And we sat for hours,
talking about what was to come.
She is nervous of the pain,
unsure of how to deal with the baby.
But I have promised her that I will be there,
that I will teach her all she needs to know.
I will help her through these next months,
the discomfort, the nerves,
the wonder of the birth.
I will see my grandchild born!

Pause

But she has not given up her grand ideas.
She tells me that her cousin is pregnant,
that this is God's child too!
Is this the new fashion,
seeing angels when pregnant?
She says they have talked and talked
about the new future,
about their babies
and how they will change the world.
But what will the future be like?

How will the world be for these two tiny lives,
and will they change it?

A candle may be lit.

O Lord, I'm nervous about the future,
not sure that I am up to keeping my promises.
Give me the strength to keep going and support those whom I love.
AMEN

Hymn – **LONG AGO, PROPHETS KNEW**
    or **ON JORDAN'S BANK THE BAPTIST'S CRY**

Reading: Luke 2: 1-7

Visual aid — bowl and towel

I am worried for my daughter.
She has had to travel so far,
and just when the baby is due.
Her husband comes from far away
and they have had to go to his home town.
It's going to be so busy,
I only hope there is somewhere for them to stay.
My poor girl!
I wanted to be with her when her time came,
I wanted to hold her hand
and stroke away her pain.
But it will not be my arms around her
as she cries out in labour,
it will not be my eyes that see my grandchild born,
or my hands that hold the child to the light.
And another voice than mine
will gladly cry "Boy" or "Girl".
It will be her husband,
and his family.

She is no longer ours, but his.
I just wish I could be there.

Pause

There is no news.
Others are returning,
but she has not.
Some tell strange tales
of a child born in a stable,
born to be king of the world.
They talk of bright stars,
and angels and shepherds.
I can only pray
"Not my girl, Lord,
  not giving birth among the straw."
And I remember her words
"This child will be great,
  and bring peace and prosperity.
  He will feed the hungry
  and give power to the down-trodden."
This cannot be her child,
my grandchild?
And others tell of massacre,
of babies killed in their beds
because of the jealousy of the king
for this child in the stable.
What can a baby do to a mighty king?

A candle may be lit.

Hymn - **BORN IN THE NIGHT**

Reading: Luke 1: 46-55

Place a cross in the centre of the display of visual aids.

Gracious God,
the God of Mary,
the God of Elizabeth,
the God of freedom and wholeness;
may your astounding and transforming love fill our lives,
taking away the smallness of our vision
and giving us the courage of Mary and Elizabeth to say,
"Yes, your kingdom come,
  your will be done."
For your name's sake, AMEN

The Lord's Prayer

Hymn – **O COME, O COME, IMMANUEL**
                or **HARK, THE HERALD ANGELS SING**
                or **O LITTLE TOWN OF BETHLEHEM**

Benediction:
May the presence of God in our lives
deepen our faith in his love
and bring us peace and understanding of those around us,
now and always. AMEN

CAROL SERVICES

All You Need For A Perfect Christmas?

CONTEXT
This carol service is a response to the message of many adverts leading up to Christmas. It examines what the advertisers tell us will make our Christmas perfect, and responds with what the message of Jesus' birth represents.

PRACTICALITIES
A nativity scene is created as each reader brings forward a figure and adds it to the display at the front. A large table, covered with a cloth, should be put where the congregation can see it.

This service works well with Posada figures, or traditional crib figures. It was first used with Fairly Traded crib figures made of recycled newspaper by people in the Philippines. This added a piquancy to the contrast with the traditions of a Western Christmas.

PEOPLE & PROPS REQUIRED
Leader

Readings:	
	Luke 1: 26-38
	Luke 2: 1-7
	Luke 8: 8-20
	Matthew 2: 1-14
	John 1:1-14, 18

Meditations:	Figures/Props:
Perfect Family Time	*Mary and Joseph*
Perfect Decorations	*Straw, Animals/Angels*
Perfect Party	*Shepherds and Angel*
Perfect Weather	*Wise men*

ALL YOU NEED FOR A PERFECT CHRISTMAS

Call to Worship: *Jeremiah 23:5-6*

CAROL – O COME ALL YE FAITHFUL (5 VERSES)

Opening prayers
Gracious God,
We come together joyfully to celebrate your birth.
With the choirs of heaven and earth we sing your praises
because you are our Saviour and our ever-loving God.

We come together joyfully to prepare our hearts
to receive you as our King
and to live our lives in the light of your Word.

We come together joyfully to listen
to your words of truth and grace
and to marvel at the wonders of your love.

We come together prayerfully
to confess the times we have overlooked your love,
have got our priorities wrong
and focussed on things which do not matter.

Open our eyes to the amazing truth
of a God who loves us so much
that he shares our human life
and open our hearts to your forgiving love
so that we can truly worship and adore you this Christmas time.
In Jesus' name we pray, **AMEN**

All you need for a perfect Christmas?
All you need for a perfect Christmas, so the advertisers tell us, is what can be bought from their client's emporium. Every Christmas they inundate us with suggestions about what we need – perfect families, perfect decorations, perfect parties, perfect weather and perfect presents. If we believe them, all we have to do is spend our money in a

particular store and we will have a hassle and trouble-free Christmas where everyone will be happy and no one will argue. If only that was true!

So that's the theme for this year's Carol Service, and that's what we're going to gather together this evening, all you need for a perfect Christmas.

But what do we need for a perfect Christmas? In a way, this links to the question with which we began Advent, what kind of King are we expecting? Because if we know what sort of King we are expecting, we know how to prepare for him. Our experience of kings on earth is that they expect perfection in people, food and places, and can be dangerously angry when they find problems. But we are not preparing for a King who expects to find perfection when he arrives because God is prepared to accept us in our ordinariness and imperfection. The gospels suggest that our King is not one who expects that everything will be done and ready but that he is prepared to roll up his sleeves and get involved with making this world into the Kingdom of Heaven, even if that means upsetting earthly rulers in the process! God upsets the mighty and brings down the powerful so that the weak and the ordinary can know that they too are loved.

CAROL - TELL OUT MY SOUL, THE GREATNESS OF THE LORD

Luke 1: 26-38

Perfect Family Time   *(Figures: Mary and Joseph)*
All you need for a perfect Christmas, so we are told, is perfect family time, and we are constantly fed images of contented children playing happily alongside calm parents and grandparents, who watch them with an indulgent smile. For how many families is this a reality? And for how many is it a distant dream because the house is filled with arguments, and over-tired children are screaming and fighting? And then there's the row over whose turn it is to wash up, and who should be doing the cooking and why there had to be cranberry sauce on the table when no

one ever eats it and who will sleep on the camp-bed in the dining room where there's a bit of a draught. Instead of the focus falling on being together, it falls on the individual who has been put out.

When you think about it, the first Christmas wasn't a perfect time for families either. Mary and Joseph weren't married and yet she was pregnant. Then she got sent away to her cousin Elizabeth in disgrace. And just when the baby was due, Mary and Joseph had to leave her family and travel to Bethlehem to register for the census and meet up with members of Joseph's family he probably hadn't seen for years. Now that is pretty much a recipe for disaster. And to cap it all, there was nowhere for them to stay other than a stable.

That puts our arguments about food and washing up to shame. But when you think about it, isn't that a wonderful thing? God didn't come to a perfect family, but to an ordinary one, with squabbles and disagreements. God didn't come as an honoured guest but had to take what was available in an overcrowded city.

The point is; Jesus is not looking for perfection, for shining, happy families. He comes to ordinary people, struggling with ordinary things, and offers them peace and hope.

CAROL - SILENT NIGHT, HOLY NIGHT

Luke 2: 1-7

Perfect Decorations   *(Figures: Straw, Angels/Animals)*
All you need for a perfect Christmas is a beautifully decorated house, all tidy and colour co-ordinated bought from an expensive store; and a huge tree dripping with ornaments and festooned with twinkling fairy lights. And on Christmas Day, a dining table set with an elegant tablecloth covered in holly leaves which only comes out once a year. Some people even like to have their houses lit up like beacons, covered in sleighs and santas and reindeer. When you drive down some streets at this time of year you get the feeling that the neighbours are in competition with one another to have the most or the brightest lights.

And this is such a contrast with the first Christmas. Think of where Jesus was born, not amid beautiful decorations with a glowing log fire and crisp, clean table linen, but in a stable, where the animals ate and slept. We know very little about the stable, all we know from Luke's account is that Jesus was laid in a manger because there was no room for them in the inn. That's because for Luke, what is really important is not where Jesus was born, but that he *was* born, that God did and does care enough about humanity to come alongside us, even in the dirtiest places, and share in the joys and pains of everyday life. For Luke, it is not the surroundings or the decorations which take centre stage, but the people, those who recognised that God was in their midst.

CAROL – CRADLED IN A MANGER MEANLY

Luke 2: 8 -20

Perfect Party   *(Figures: Shepherds and Angel)*
All you need for the perfect Christmas is a perfect party. It's the time of year for parties, work parties, family parties, parties at the pub, a great time for getting together. And if the supermarkets are to be believed, all you need for a perfect party are their delicious range of party snacks, so easily prepared that you have all the time in world to pamper yourself with their exclusive range of clothing and toiletries. But what is a party without guests? How long do people agonise over the perfect guest list? Of course, there are the works' Christmas parties where the guest list is simple, everyone who works in one department, but then, there's the vital choice to be made about where you sit – near the boss and look like a creep, or with the people you like, or the people who could be useful to you? And what about family parties, or parties with friends? Do you invite the people you know you should invite or those you like or who might invite you to their party in return? It's the guest list which really tells you what or who is important to the host.

So the guest list at Jesus' birth is rather surprising. The first visitors are not the dignitaries of the town, or those who needed to be impressed, but the dirty, smelly shepherds who have not bothered to wash and change but have come straight down from the hills to the stable. They were generally not well-educated men and are not likely to have had the best table manners, and yet they were welcomed as friends, rather than frowned upon as intruders. And that tells us that all God wants for a perfect Christmas is that we are as eager as the shepherds, and as welcoming as Mary and Joseph.

CAROL – WHILE SHEPHERDS WATCHED THEIR FLOCKS BY NIGHT

Matthew 2: 1-14

Perfect Weather   *(Figures: Wise Men)*

All you need for a perfect Christmas is snow, deep and crisp and even. Have you noticed that on all the adverts for Christmas it is snowing? And that the snow makes everyone happy and rosy-cheeked, no mention of the cold, or the isolation, or the inconvenience of getting stuck many miles from home? The perfect Christmas, according to the advertisers, is a White Christmas, where treetops glisten and children listen to hear sleigh bells in the snow. The truth is that snow makes life very much more difficult, or lonely, or frightening for very many people. Travelling is difficult, we realise how much we have come to rely on our cars, or having shops conveniently stocked with everything we need. And everything takes so much more effort in the snow because it's harder to walk through and you're in danger of slipping over on the ice, and you have to wrap up in several layers of clothing before you even go out of the door.

But if it's difficult for us, how much more difficult would it have been in first century Palestine? They wouldn't have had 4x4s or snow ploughs or even salt and grit. Yet those travellers from the East persisted with their journey, probably for many months, because they believed that the baby they would find in Bethlehem was worth the effort, was worth bothering with, because he was God's way of saying that we are worth bothering with.

CAROL – IN THE BLEAK MIDWINTER

Perfect Presents   *(Leader)*

All you need for a perfect Christmas is a perfect present. How much time have you spent this year looking for it? Browsing through catalogues, searching websites, traipsing around shops? Or do your family and friends work on "lists", subtly left lying around in case anyone is interested in what to get you? And then you can't find what's on the lists, or it's more than you wanted to pay, and you don't want to look like a skinflint but is there anything cheaper that you can afford? Then when you've bought it, you've got to wrap it and get it there in time for Christmas. Some people enjoy wrapping and spend hours with ribbons and colour co-ordinated paper, and others can only wrap square boxes and have to rely on miles of Sellotape to make it stay in one piece.

And then there's the minefield of the present-opening itself, especially if it's in front of the person who's bought it for you. You don't want to look too eager as if you are expecting something in case you don't get anything, and you can't look too disappointed if it's not what you wanted, or it's too big or too small. And after all the hassle, you think that the perfect present is just a figment of the advertisers' imagination.

And yet, it isn't.

The perfect gift is freedom from the expectation to be perfect. God does not expect us to be perfect, to get everything right all the time, but rather to be live lives full of love and forgiveness for others.

The origins of the Posada nativity figures we have used tonight are in the poor villages of Mexico, where they struggle to make ends meet. Any Christmas celebrations they have would not measure up to our standards of perfection. They can barely afford to feed their family, never mind worrying about who's doing the washing up, or what to do with the leftover turkey. They do not have expensive Christmas decorations, are never invited to parties, and if they went, they would be turned away as dirty beggars and, whatever the weather they have to live in tiny shacks that we would shudder to use as garden sheds. Yet, through the lives of these people God shines the light of truth by showing us that Christmas is not about baubles and tinsel, or perfect families or friends, or the newest and best of everything, but about love and redemption, offering hospitality and care to those whom others have turned away.

Our nativity scene reminds us that two thousand years ago God came as a baby to a poor family, to live amongst the outcast and the dispossessed, to show that we are all worth bothering with and that each of us is capable of living a beautiful and meaningful life, when we take seriously the challenge of Immanuel, God with us.

This means that the perfect gifts are love and forgiveness because, when they are freely given, they help us to love ourselves and to let go of past hurts and arguments, and to see the value of all people, even those whom society says are not perfect.

Love tells us that we are not alone, and forgiveness accepts us with all our faults.

You can't wrap these gifts in coloured paper and ribbons, nor can they be bought online. They are the perfect presents not only because they never wear out, but because they bring joy and fullness of life to both the giver and the receiver.

God offers us love, forgiveness and understanding in Jesus Christ, not wrapped up in beautiful ribbons, but in a human being, who came to share our human life, to show us what perfect love is, to teach us the way of forgiveness and to redeem us into the beauty of God's Kingdom.

So all you need for a perfect Christmas is a heart that is open to receive the love, forgiveness and understanding of God, and to see the grace of God in the face of a child.

John 1: 1-14, 18

CAROL – O LITTLE TOWN OF BETHLEHEM

Prayers of Intercession

"We pray,
Shine your light of hope into their lives."

Loving God, you came as a child to a poor family,
we remember those families who struggle to be together without
    fighting;
for those who will spend Christmas away from their homes and families;
and for those in the family of nations who are affected by war,
starvation and conflict.

We pray,
Shine your light of hope into their lives.

Loving God, you came to an outhouse rather than to a beautifully
    decorated home,
we remember those who live in poverty,
who struggle to find money to pay for heating, or food, or clothes
and for whom Christmas merely adds to the stress and the worry.

We pray,
Shine your light of hope into their lives.

Loving God, you welcomed the most unlikely people to parties
we remember those for whom Christmas is a lonely time,
those who live alone, who have been bereaved
or who are ill in hospital or at home.

We pray,
Shine your light of hope into their lives.

Loving God, you created the wind and calmed the storm
we remember those caught up in extremes of weather
those affected by the snow and unable to get out
those affected by drought, or flood or earthquakes.

We pray,
Shine your light of hope into their lives.

Loving God,
We all stand in need of your gifts of love and forgiveness
Shine your light of hope into our lives, we pray
For the sake of Jesus Christ, our Lord
AMEN

The Lord's Prayer

Offering

CAROL – HARK! THE HERALD ANGELS SING

Benediction
May the love of God, the peace of the Christ-child and the insight of the
Holy Spirit overflow our hearts this Christmastime and for evermore.
AMEN

Bethlehem

CONTEXT

The inspiration for this Carol Service came from the images of Bethlehem on the television news and realising how different they were from the words "O little town of Bethlehem, how still we see thee lie." Although the initial idea had been to contrast the current reality of life in Bethlehem with the typical nativity scenes, it grew into a reflection on how much we take the words of carols for granted. This prompted two questions, how would we react if Jesus was born in our "little town" and what would happen if we took the words of the carols seriously. So there are two threads running through this service – realising that Bethlehem was an ordinary town, much like the places in which we live, and the words of carols that have a should have a serious impact on our Christian living.

PRACTICALITIES

The name of the town in which this service is being used needs to be substituted for the one where it was initially used, and similarly the year needs to be changed. They are bracketed and in italics to make them easy to identify.

PEOPLE NEEDED
Leader

Readings:	Micah 5: 5-8	Meditations:	In Bethlehem was born
	Luke 2: 1-7		In a cattle shed
	Luke 2: 8-20		The First Apostles
	Matthew 2: 1-13		Kneel in homage
	John 1: 1-14		

BETHLEHEM

Call to Worship
We have come, as the faithful of all ages have gathered,
to hear again the story of the birth of the saviour,
to draw near to Christ's cradle
and to share in the choirs of angels.
We have come to worship and adore the True God and Light of all,
who comes to us in humility and love.

CAROL – HARK, THE HERALD ANGELS SING

Opening Prayers (based on Hark, the herald angels sing)
Almighty God,
as we listen again for the choirs of angels,
we are reminded to praise you for your marvellous works.
Even in difficult and troubled times,
we see your peace on earth,
and trust that through faith in you
all things will be made whole.
Through your great mercy
you offer forgiveness and reconciliation for all.
Joyfully, with all the nations,
we open our hearts to you in praise and worship.

Loving Christ,
adored by the highest heaven,
we celebrate your great love for us
shown in the way you laid by your glory
and became flesh to share our human life,
to live that we no more may die,
and to demonstrate the reality
of Immanuel, God with us.
Joyfully, with all the nations,
we open our hearts to you in praise and worship.

Creative Spirit, bringer of light and life,
we praise you for the way you inspire us
leading us to new life and offering us healing,
encouraging us to see God at work in all things.
Joyfully, with all the nations,
we open our hearts to you in praise and worship.

Eternal God, Father, Son and Holy Spirit,
for all you have done, are doing and will do for us,
Joyfully, with all the nations,
we open our hearts to offer you our praise and worship.
For Jesus' sake, **AMEN**

Introduction
Welcome to this carol service in which we will hear the familiar Christmas story and sing again some of our favourite carols. The focus of this service is the place which was the centre of all the activity – Bethlehem, which was an ordinary little town, not unlike (*Thirsk*), full of people doing ordinary jobs and living ordinary lives, just like us. We shall be looking at various phrases in the carols and using them to help us reflect on the meaning of Jesus' birth at the first Christmas to the people of Bethlehem, and to us and the ordinary people of our own town, now in (*2013*).

CAROL – TELL OUT MY SOUL, THE GREATNESS OF THE LORD

Micah 5: 5-8

"In Bethlehem was born"
We're used to the name Bethlehem, it doesn't surprise us. It's well-known as the birth-place of Jesus. But to most people in the time of Jesus it would be like saying to someone from another part of this country, "I come from (*Thirsk, North Yorkshire*)" to which we normally get the response "Where?" or "Oh yes, (*Herriot*) country", just as first century Palestinians would have said "Oh yes, King David's town".

This was because Bethlehem was just an ordinary town, a forgotten town but for a famous former resident. Micah describes it as "the least of the cities of Judah", so it wasn't very important. It was just a place where people went about their daily lives, doing their jobs as they had always done.

Its one claim to fame was that the youngest son of a local family had been a shepherd boy who fought the Philistines and grew up to become a famous king, but that was a thousand years ago. There were no blue plaques by which to remember him, no tourist shops selling souvenirs, just an ordinary place where people got on with their lives.

Bethlehem wasn't a place for powerful people, they lived in Jerusalem. Nor was it a place for rich people, they lived in the country, away from the smells of other people in the city. Bethlehem was an ordinary place for ordinary people, like *(Thirsk, or Sowerby or Ripon)*.

CAROL - IT CAME UPON A MIDNIGHT CLEAR

Luke 2: 1-7

"In a cattle shed"
Almost everyone had a cattle shed, somewhere to keep the animals at night. Some people even kept their animals in their own homes. Whilst the humans slept on a platform in the house, the animals slept on the floor! So it wasn't such an unusual place to find a bed for the night.

The problem is, we're used to homes with vacuum cleaners and where animals are kept outside, and the idea of sleeping in the same room as them is a bit strange. It offends our twenty first century ideas of hygiene and health and safety.

But the point of it is, it was a very ordinary place then, not in a royal palace, or a separate room, but the meeting place for everyone, where everyone, including the animals, lived. Jesus was born into the middle of life, into the middle of ordinary life. He was not marked out as special because of where he was, or because his parents were rich or famous.

Jesus was special because his place of birth was ordinary, his parents were ordinary, because he shows us that God thinks that ordinary people are special enough to care for and to die for.

CAROL – SILENT NIGHT, HOLY NIGHT

Luke 2: 8-20

"The First Apostles of His Infant Fame"
The shepherds are an unlikely crowd
to be counted as apostles.
Ragged, dirty outcast
from village and family.

Not rich courtiers in fine clothing
or heralds from a palace
in livery and pomp
announcing the birth
of the King of Creation.

No, huddled round a fire for warmth,
telling jokes, swapping stories,
keeping away the cold
and the fear of wild animals,
these unlikely heralds,
chosen by God
showed honest, open faith,
trust and humility.

And that's the secret of God's revolution.
God's love comes to ordinary people,
it is not earned with wealth
or influence
or goodness,
but given in grace and love.

And these "first apostles of his infant fame"
they trusted God's grace and love and were glad.

CAROL – CRADLED IN A MANGER MEANLY

Matthew 2: 1-13

"Kneel in homage"
This is a bit of an old-fashioned phrase.
We don't talk about doing homage to people any more.
We idolise celebrities,
and then we do our best to destroy them.
We envy their riches
and then convince ourselves that they don't bring happiness.
because we are jealous of their success.

That is not homage.
It is greed and envy and jealousy.

Homage comes from the same root word as humility.
Humility means recognising our own limits
Homage means being thankful to those who show us how to overcome
        them.
It means being able to recognise that someone is better than we are,
and not envying them
or trying to destroy them.

It is simple joy in their ability
without asking what they can do for us.
It is simple joy that their lives have touched ours
and that we have been privileged to share it.

Homage comes from love
which is never jealous, or arrogant, or rude.
And love
is what we celebrate
in the birth of Jesus Christ

And these rich travellers, in fine clothes
have travelled miles and have not ended up,
in the grand palace they expected.

Yet still they kneel in homage,
on the dirty floor of the stable,
because they recognise the greatness of God,
and the way this child is going to revolutionise the world.

CAROL - O LITTLE TOWN OF BETHLEHEM

The Real Bethlehem   *(Leader)*

Have you ever noticed how much licence the writers of the carols take with the Christmas story? They add in all sorts of characters and details which are not actually in the biblical text. For example, the First Nowell has the three magi visiting the baby in the stable, when in Matthew's gospel it quite clearly states that they were in a house. Can you imagine a crib scene without a little donkey, but that would have been a most impractical way for a pregnant woman to travel? Several carols talk about the presence of angels at the stable, when there is no mention of them in Luke or Matthew. And what about the time of year? Many carols talk about snow and the bleak mid-winter, yet actually that would not have been a sensible time for an emperor to call a census, because the bad weather makes travelling so difficult, and the shepherds would not have been out in the fields because the sheep would have been brought close into the town for the winter. One man, when confronted with this during a Bible Study, complained that his Christmas had been completely ruined!

And what about the focus of our thoughts this morning, Bethlehem? Described by the carol writers as little, still, Royal, celebrated, and yet, what do we see on the news and in the newspapers? The wall that runs down the West Bank cuts Bethlehem off from Jerusalem and divides families. There are frequent injuries and occasional deaths in the town because of fighting between Palestinian and Israeli forces. Is this town really peaceful and Royal? And actually, because it lies in the borders with other territories, it has never been so. It has always been a place of conflicting territorial claims, where people may be frightened to walk around alone. Because of human pride and ego, there is no peace, and there can be no dreamless sleep, for the dream is always of peace which never comes.

So the Middle East has never been a particularly peaceful place, and it is deeply saddening that it is still in turmoil today. Despite what the carol tells us, the little town of Bethlehem has never lain still in the moonlight, there is always unrest. And today, (*Syria, Libya, Egypt)*, are all in turmoil, and there is unrest in (*Afghanistan and Iraq*). God shows us the way of peace by laying aside power, majesty and influence to be born as a helpless child in a borrowed stable. We may not be able to solve the problems of the wars of the world, but we can pray and work for God's peace where we are, with the ordinary people we meet, just as the shepherds did.

So we take off the rose-tinted glasses of the writers of the carols, and we are faced with a God who chose to come to earth, not to a royal city, not to a place where he would be welcomed and cosseted with open arms, but to a forgotten city, where there was difficulty and trouble. He did not come to a perfect world to be worshipped, but to a broken world to heal it.

And what does this mean for Bethlehem, for us, in (*2013)*? That God comes to ordinary places and people, not the extraordinary, that we do not have to be perfect to be loved by God, and that he can come into the most broken and difficult places, uninvited, quietly, and transform them with his love, peace, joy and hope.

John 1: 1-14

Offering

CAROL – WHO WOULD THINK THAT WHAT WAS NEEDED?

Prayers of Intercession
"Loving God,
Hear our prayers for your world."

We have been reminded that God comes to ordinary people and gives meaning and purpose to every life, so let us pray for those in need in God's world.

Eternal God,
We have been reminded that the angels sang of Peace on Earth,
so we pray for the people in this world who do not know peace because they are surrounded by war and violence.   May they be released from fear and set free to live their lives in joy.

> Loving God,
> **Hear our prayers for your world.**

We pray for the leaders who can bring peace, but are afraid of appearing weak or are too proud to admit that they are wrong. Give them humility and a desire for peace.

> Loving God,
> **Hear our prayers for your world.**

We have been reminded that your Son was born away from home, in a room lent by a stranger,
so we pray for those who are homeless, living in doorways, or on rubbish tips, afraid of the cold, unsure of where they will find the next meal.

> Loving God,
> **Hear our prayers for your world.**

We pray for the charities and organisations who work with the homeless to find them somewhere safe and warm to sleep, and offer them hot meals. We remember especially the work of Crisis at Christmas.

> Loving God,
> **Hear our prayers for your world.**

We have been reminded of that Mary sang about your plan to save the world by freeing the captives and the oppressed;
so we pray for those who are in prison, separated from their families and struggling with new experiences. We pray too for those who are

oppressed, by an unfair regime, or pressures of work, or addiction. Help them to find peace, and a way to freedom and new life.

Loving God,
Hear our prayers for your world.

Eternal God,
Help us to sing your song
of love and peace come down
so that the light of your coming Kingdom will dawn,
for your name's sake, we pray. **AMEN**

The Lord's Prayer

CAROL - HARK THE HERALD ANGELS SING

Benediction
May the love of God,
God who comes to ordinary people
and ordinary places,
fill our hearts with hope, peace and joy
this Christmastime and for evermore. **AMEN**

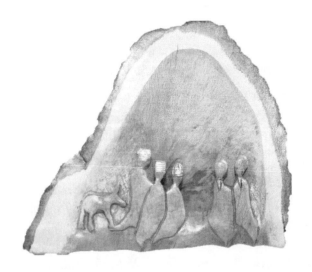

Counterbalance

CONTEXT
The idea of this service is to show that although many of the traditions and cultural expectations of Christmas create stress and arguments, this is counterbalanced by the message of peace Jesus brings. It works well with one person reading the words of the prophet, especially if they can sit somewhere prominent such as the pulpit whilst the leader responds with "God, through the baby in the manger" at the end of each meditation. Readers should be asked to remain at the front until the next carol begins to avoid disturbance during the pause and the response of the Leader.

PRACTICALITIES
Each of the five "characters" have an object to bring forward and place on the table before beginning their monologue. They also have their keyword, which they attach to the display as they mention it. The leader places the counterbalance word opposite the keyword before they read the sentence "God, through the baby in the manger..." The final result should look like the image below. This can be done with either a display board and pins or using PowerPoint.

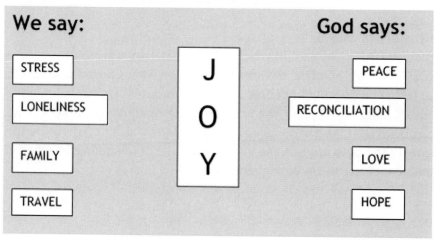

PEOPLE REQUIRED

Leader

Prophet

Readings:	Luke 2: 1-7	*Meditations:*	Joseph
	Luke 2: 8-20		Innkeeper's wife
	John 1: 1-14		Wise man
			Mary's mother
			Mary

PROPS REQUIRED

Character	Object	Keyword	Counter balance
Joseph	Statue of Holy Family	Stress	Peace
Innkeeper's wife	Tray of crockery	Family	Love
Wise man	OS Map	Travel	Hope
Mary's mother	Photo in frame	Loneliness	Reconciliation
Mary	Hymnbook	Joy	

COUNTERBALANCE

Introduction

Welcome to this service in which we celebrate again the birth of Christ 2000 years ago and take the time to reflect on what Christmas means to us by hearing again the desires expressed in our liturgy for lighting the advent candles. Through the words of bible readings, meditations and carols we will take a fresh look at this well-known story as we re-live the story of the birth of Jesus and encounter some of the people involved in that first Christmas in Bethlehem.

Call to Worship: verses from John 1
The Word became flesh and lived among us:
We have seen his glory, the glory of the one and only Son
　　　who came from the Father, full of grace and truth.

CAROL – HARK THE HERALD ANGELS SING

Opening Prayers
Living God,
Creator of all things, Lover of all creation,
We praise and thank you for your goodness
Your grace, your truth and your love
Shown to us in Jesus Christ your son
Who came to earth,
Was born in a stable,
Lived amongst the poor,
Was put to death on a cross,
And raised to new life with you, for us.
For this love, we praise and worship you, for ever. **AMEN**

Luke 2: 1-7

CAROL - THE ANGEL GABRIEL FROM HEAVEN CAME

Prophet:　　　The word of God came to Isaiah, son of Amoz:
　　　　　　　"The Lord himself will give you a sign: A virgin shall
　　　　　　　conceive and bear a son and call him Emmanuel, God
　　　　　　　with us."

Joseph (wound up)　　　　　　　　　　　　　　　　　*(statue)*
You want the word that sums up my Christmas? STRESS. *(Puts "Stress" on display)* I'm Joseph, husband of Mary, as in Mary and … Not that I get much of a mention in the Christmas story, even though I was there working away in the background all the time, just the strong silent type, keeping in the shadows, out of sight.

The stress seemed to be never-ending. What do you think it was like for me, preparing for a baby to be born, with all the neighbours looking on and commenting? There always seemed to be things needing to be done, and just when I thought it was all sorted out, there was a last minute change of plan and I had to get myself and Mary to Bethlehem, instead of having a quiet time at home, and Mary was in no fit state to walk, so I had to go out and borrow a donkey!

And then there was the stress of the journey, walking alongside the donkey, plodding along, worried about Mary's health and what was going to happen to the baby. Every night when we stopped, I had to find somewhere for her to sleep that was comfortable and warm, and find some food.

And then, with all the stops we had to make so that Mary was comfortable, we arrived at Bethlehem so late that there was nowhere left to stay, and I had to plead with any number of relatives before I got the use of an outhouse. And before we could use it, I had to clean it and make up beds from the straw, because Mary wasn't in any fit state to do it. Then just as I was drifting off to sleep, thinking that all my worries were over at last, Mary shook me awake to tell me that the baby was coming, now. There was no one around at that time of night, so I had to deliver the baby myself, whilst keeping Mary calm and comfortable. Then just as I had got her and the baby settled, we were inundated with visitors, shepherds, wise men, the innkeeper's wife – where were they when I needed them? I was exhausted, but all they did was coo over the baby and Mary.

So yes, stress, that's what my Christmas was about.

Pause

Leader: And God, through the baby in the manger says:
              "Peace I leave with you, my peace I give to you. Do not
              be troubled and upset." *(John 14: 27)*
                                        (Places "Peace" on the display)

94

CAROL - CRADLED IN A MANGER MEANLY

Prophet: The word of God came to Isaiah, son of Amoz.

"To us a child is born, to us a son is given and the government will be upon his shoulders. He will be called the Wonderful Counsellor, Almighty God, Everlasting Father, Prince of Peace"

Innkeeper's wife (Bustling, busy)   *(Tray of crockery)*

My word for Christmas is "family" (*places "Family" on display*). Oh yes, we've all heard that, haven't we, Christmas is a time for families, well mine was, in abundance. You see, my husband and I run a small guest house in Bethlehem, nothing fancy, but it earns us a living. We were in the quiet season, enjoying a bit of a rest when the Roman emperor dropped a census on us. We were lucky, my husband comes from Bethlehem so we didn't have to travel anywhere, but we were inundated with people wanting to stay with us, all claiming to be relatives – well you know what it's like in these country places, everyone's related to everyone else. And they were all saying "You must remember me, I'm your second cousin's second cousin" or something equally stupid, and suddenly, after years of not seeing them or hearing from them, they expected me to find somewhere for them to stay, and they thought that as they were family they wouldn't have to pay for it! And on top of that, I had to find enough food to feed them all, and enough plates and cups to go round! It was a bit much really, but my husband's too soft, and let them all come in. He was run ragged, trying to keep them all fed and watered, but enjoying seeing the inn so full and catching up with all his family. Late on one evening there was a knock at the door, and my husband went to answer it. I shouted to him from the kitchen that if it was any more of his family he was to tell them to try some other mug. I didn't hear what happened at the door, but no one else came in, so I was relieved, and didn't think anything of the fact that my husband then went straight out to the stable.

When things quietened down a bit later on, I asked him who was at the door, and he told me about this young couple, expecting a child, and how he couldn't turn them away so he had ended up putting them in an outhouse. I was going to give him a large piece of my mind, when I heard a noise out in the street. I looked out and saw these shepherds walking towards our stable. What did those lowlifes think they were doing in our town, even in the middle of the night? I turned to my husband and told him to get rid of them, but he just said "Leave them be, they aren't doing any harm." But I couldn't do that, we had a house full of family, couldn't let them think that we allowed that sort of people to hang around our house, so I went round to the stable to have it out with them. The young couple in there didn't seem to mind, in fact the mother seemed to welcome them, although her husband looked a bit stressed. The shepherds were spinning her some tale about an angel who told them to come and visit the baby. What sort of fairy story is that? I stood and watched them for a moment, she was utterly caught up in her baby, her first, and the shepherds were quiet, no cursing like they usually do, and I didn't want to interrupt, it looked so peaceful. But I couldn't understand what all the fuss was about. I mean, I know every woman thinks her first child is God's gift, but what did these shepherds, normally so caught up with their sheep and lambs, see in this smelly stable to make them think so too?

Pause

Leader: God through the baby in the manger says:
                "God himself loves you, because you have loved me and
                have believed that I came from God." *(John 16:25)*
                                        (Puts "Love" on the display)

CAROL – AWAY IN A MANGER

Luke 2: 8-20

CAROL - WHILE SHEPHERDS WATCHED

Prophet: The word of God came to Micah of Moresheth:
"Bethlehem, of Ephrathah, who are one of the least of the clans of Judah, from you shall come forth for me one who is to rule in Israel, whose origin is from of old. He will stand and shepherd his flock in the strength of the Lord."

Wise Man (tired, ponderous)   *(OS map)*
I'm so tired. We've been travelling for days. (*Puts "Travel" on display*) There were times I thought we would never get here! My friends and I have spent years following the stars and reading the prophecies. We never thought that we would see one of them come true. Many months ago, I saw the portents in the stars, and went to see my fellow seers. We looked at the prophecy of Micah again, and again, and eventually decided that we had to set out to try and find Bethlehem. We travelled for many weeks, and through unknown countries, where we were baffled by their customs, not sure what to do or say next, uncomfortable in unfamiliar surroundings. And all the way we were asking ourselves if we were right, was it going to be worth it, or was it all going to be a waste of time and effort?

Sometimes as we travelled we discussed the gifts we had brought – gold, frankincense and myrrh. They seemed to be strange gifts to bring to a baby, even a baby king. We knew that the gold was a symbol of kingship, and the frankincense was understandable if he was the leader of the national religion, but myrrh, wasn't that a bit premature, or was he going to die young?

But stranger still was where he was born, not in Herod's royal palace where we looked for him first, but in a stable, amongst ordinary people, the poor and the outcasts. What sort of a king was this?

Pause

Leader:	And God, through the baby in the manger says
	"I have come to bring good news to the poor,
	to proclaim release for the captives
	and recovery of sight to the blind,
	to let the oppressed go free,
	and to proclaim the year of the Lord's favour."

(Luke 4: 16-20)   *(Places "Hope" on display)*

CAROL - LOVE CAME DOWN AT CHRISTMAS

Prophet:	The word of God came to Jeremiah, son of Hilkiah.
	"Because of the Lord's great love we are not consumed,
	for his compassions never fail.
	They are new every morning; great is God's faithfulness."

Mary's mother (Wistful)   *(framed photo)*

I'm Anne, Mary's mother, left behind in Nazareth, when I want to be with Mary. It's my first grandchild, and I wanted to be there, with my daughter, to help her. Perhaps it's my own fault. I shouldn't have gone on at her so much before she left, told her that she was a disgrace to us all and that she was throwing her life away.

How I wish I hadn't said that now.

All I want is to be there with her. I've spent so much time just sitting and wondering what's happening in Bethlehem, has she had the baby, what does he look like, that I haven't done anything here. One of my neighbours called round today and I was so ashamed at the state of the house that I couldn't let her in. But what did happen in Bethlehem? Was Joseph able to help, where are they staying? But I'm not needed any more, my child has grown up, got a family of her own, and I'm just left alone with my thoughts and my memories.

So yes, loneliness, that's what sums up my Christmas, the loneliness of not being needed and forgotten by my family. *(Puts "Loneliness" on the display)*

Pause

Leader: But God, through the baby in the manger says:
           "I am with you always, even to the end of the age."
           (Matthew 28:20)   *(Places "Reconciliation" on display)*

CAROL – BORN IN THE NIGHT

Prophet: The word of God came to Jeremiah, son of Hilkiah.
              "The days are coming, declares the Lord, when I will raise
              up to David a righteous branch, a King who will reign
              wisely and do what is just and right in the land."

Mary (Joyful)

I'm Mary, and the only word that sums up my Christmas is joy. *(Puts joy in the centre of the display)* I'm so full of joy that I just want to sing out in praise to God.

O, how my soul praises the Lord.
How my spirit rejoices in God my Saviour!
For he took notice of this lowly servant girl,
and from now on all generations will call me blessed.
For the Mighty One has done great things for me
And holy is His name.
His mercy is for those who fear him from generation to generation
He has shown strength with his arm
He has scattered the proud in the thoughts of their hearts
He has brought down the powerful from their thrones,
and lifted up the lowly.
He has filled the hungry with good things
and the rich he has sent empty away."

CAROL – SEE AMID THE WINTER'S SNOW

John 1: 1-14

Prayers of intercession

Leader: We bring to God our concerns for the world and for the people we meet as we say our prayers.

Let us pray:

Jesus Christ, Word of God, you come to bring peace to the world, so we pray for those who are stressed at work or at home, because they are caring for loved ones at home or in hospital, or trying to keep things together when it feels like life is falling apart. We pray for those whose work is often overlooked and who feel ignored.

Silence

Pour your words of peace into their lives this Christmas.

Jesus Christ, Word of God, you come to bring love to the world, so we pray for those whose love is stretched to the limit or abused, for those who misunderstand what love really means and hurt others with their thoughtlessness.

Silence

Pour your words of love into their lives this Christmas

Jesus Christ, Word of God, you come to bring hope to the world, so we pray for those who are travelling, on long and short journeys, to unknown places wondering what they will find at the end of the road. We remember especially those who are refugees, escaping persecution and war, uncertain of what the future holds for them.

Silence

Pour your words of hope into their lives this Christmas

Jesus Christ, Word of God, you come to bring forgiveness to the world, so we pray for those who are lonely and estranged from those whom they love, unable to make peace with them. We remember those areas of the world where there is conflict and war with lives lost and people injured.

Silence

Pour your words of forgiveness into their lives this Christmas.

Jesus Christ, Word of God, you come to bring joy to the world.
May your love make our hearts overflow with joy as we celebrate your birth and human life in Jesus so that others may hear the good news of your love for all people.
In Jesus' name we ask this **AMEN**

Offering

CAROL – JOY TO THE WORLD

Benediction
God of joy, hope, peace and love,
We praise you for the gifts you bring to us
For your love and hope which fill our hearts
And your joy and peace which light up our lives.
May your words and gifts live in us this Christmastime and for evermore.
AMEN

Joy To The World

CONTEXT
This service is one of those examples of necessity as the genesis of invention. The Choir Leader had decided that they would sing a carol from New Zealand that he had found. The trouble was, it would not fit into a traditional carol service as it did not make reference to the gospel stories, or anything that could be related to them. The problem was resolved by looking not at the carols but at their origins, and by turning to John 3:16 "God so loved the world…" What developed was a reminder that God is not limited to our experience and that Jesus touched and still touches lives across the whole world, not just in one community.

PRACTICALITIES
This service is one that lends itself to PowerPoint images of the parts of the world being visited. The recurring motif is Isaiah 9: 2-7, which could also be woven into the images displayed, particularly during the prayers of intercession.

PEOPLE REQUIRED
Leader

Readings:	Isaiah 9: 2-7	Meditations:	Do we really need a Saviour?
	Luke 1: 26-38		Kneel before him
	Luke 2: 1-7		The Simple Things
	Luke 2: 8-20		
	John 1: 1-14		

JOY TO THE WORLD

Welcome
Welcome to our Carol Service in which we celebrate the birth of our Saviour. This service is a little different because it takes us on a world tour as we visit the places in which the authors of carols lived, and what inspired them to write their carols.

Call to Worship
Come, come to worship,
Come and worship the new-born King.
Come and marvel at God in human form,
Come and worship the new-born King.
Come, come to see
Love come down at Christmas
Come and worship the new-born King.

Our first destination is France with Angels from the Realms of Glory. Whilst the words are English, it set to an old French folk tune. The words invite people from across the world to come and worship the new-born king.

CAROL - ANGELS FROM THE REALMS OF GLORY

Introduction (Leader)
At Christmas time we can become very wrapped up in what is going on in our own part of the world –have we got all the presents? Have we forgotten to send anyone a Christmas card? Will the turkey be big enough? Will it cook properly?

We need to be reminded that God created and loves the whole world, the world which comes to us through our television screens and the pages of the newspapers. John 3:16 tells us that God so loved the world, that he sent his only begotten Son. This is the reason we're looking at Christmas carols from around the world to remind ourselves that we are part of God's created world, and that we are called to work alongside Christians across the whole world.

So let us pray to God, and give thanks for the light that shines in the world, and the love that keeps it shining:

Opening Prayers
Eternal God, we give you thanks
for sending light into the darkened world;
the light of peace in the darkness of war
the light of hope in the darkness of despair
the light of truth in the face of deceit
and the light of joy in your presence.

We give you thanks
for demonstrating your grace;
not just to us,
but to the whole world.
Remind us of the grace that forgives
renews and upholds us
and those we find it hard to forgive.

We give you thanks
for the new life you offer
through the vulnerability of a new-born child,
through the life of an outcast
through the love that bears all things
including death on a cross
to bring us to new life.

We give you thanks
Eternal God,
for the light, grace and life you bring to our lives.
By the power of your Holy Spirit
help us to embrace them
and share them in your world.
For your name's sake. **AMEN**

Our next carol comes from America. It was written by Phillips Brooks, who was a minister in Philadelphia during and after the American Civil War. He went on a trip to the Holy Land, and he was inspired to write this carol after a horseback ride from Jerusalem to Bethlehem where he helped at Midnight Mass, in 1865. He wrote the following about the journey.

> "I remember standing in the old church in Bethlehem, close to the spot where Jesus was born, when the whole church was ringing hour after hour with splendid hymns of praise to God, how again and again it seemed as if I could hear voices I knew well, telling each other of the Wonderful Night of the Saviour's birth."

CAROL - O LITTLE TOWN OF BETHLEHEM

Isaiah 9: 2-7 - The Promise of a Saviour

Do we really need a Saviour?
The world doesn't need a Saviour
we're doing all right on our own.
We don't need a Wonderful Counsellor
someone interfering
and telling us what to do.

There are enough leaders in this world
without another one
full of their own importance
and causing divisions with their opinions.
And if that is not what the Mighty God is like
who will listen?
No one follows a vulnerable leader.

We don't need a Saviour
We've found ways of curing diseases
and replacing missing limbs,
and forestalling death.

We are greater than our Fathers,
than any Father however eternal.

What can a Saviour teach us?
We have discovered the secrets
of the world around us.
We've split the atom
and broken the sound barrier.
We are greater than any Prince of Peace,
There is nothing we cannot do.
Except stop violence, terrorism, war, oppression, inequality...

What more could a Saviour do?
Reveal truth?
Heal guilt?
Bring forgiveness?
Teach us to love our neighbours?

We don't need a Saviour
....do we?

For our next carol, we move to the Basque region, a mountainous area in the Pyrenees between France and Spain, a region which sees itself as occupied by a foreign power and where traditions and native languages are suppressed. This is very much what was happening to the Jewish people at the time of Jesus' birth, as they struggled against Roman occupation.

CAROL - THE ANGEL GABRIEL FROM HEAVEN CAME

Luke 1: 26-38 The Angel visits Mary

Mary then went on to visit Elizabeth her cousin and they together praised God for their part in God's coming to earth. Mary sang the Magnificat, the hymn which tells of God's purpose for his world, a setting of which we sing in our next carol.

CAROL – TELL OUT MY SOUL, THE GREATNESS OF THE LORD

Luke 2: 1-7 – The Birth in Bethlehem

The story behind the writing of the next carol has become something of a legend – how the priest at Oberndorf was horrified to find that the organ wouldn't work, and how he turned to his friend Franz Gruber to ask him to write a carol which could be accompanied by a guitar, and *Silent Night* was the result. More recently, it gained a new significance as soldiers who fought in World War One recalled how on Christmas Eve 1914, the carol could be heard coming from the German trenches, and was the beginning of the famous Christmas truce. Truly there was heavenly peace then.

CAROL - SILENT NIGHT

Luke 2: 8-20

What else could we sing now, but While Shepherds watched their flocks by night? The writer of the carol, Nahum Tate was Irish, and was born and brought up in Dublin. He was very involved in the metrification of the psalms like turning Psalm 100 into "All people that on earth do dwell" meaning that people could sing them rather than saying them. This made them more memorable and encouraged the illiterate labourers to feel that the Bible was for them as well as for those who could read it for themselves. He wrote this carol to re-tell the story we've just heard from Luke's gospel.

CAROL - WHILE SHEPHERDS WATCHED THEIR FLOCKS

Matthew 2: 1-12

Kneeling before him
Many of the carols that tell the story of the arrival of the wise men focus on the way they followed the star, or on the significance of the gifts they brought with them. None of them mention the minor detour to Herod's palace in Jerusalem, or the tragedy that followed that mistake.

Yet the incredible thing about this part of the Christmas story is that these were learned men, revered in their own country. They risked their reputations and their lives to visit the place where Jesus was born.

And when they arrived, after a long journey, they would have been stiff, tired and saddle-sore. They probably wanted a comfortable seat, rather than to kneel on the hard floor of a dirty stable.

Yet they knelt, and worshipped.

In that simple action we see humility and grace. They made themselves vulnerable to exploitation and attack. But they were so amazed by the light and grace they encountered in God revealed in vulnerability and love that they knelt and worshipped.

It is not the gifts, or the star that are the most wonderful part of the story, it is that powerful, influential men knelt in humility, not jostling for position, but simply knelt together, and worshipped.

The challenge to us is to do the same, put aside jealousy, competition and pride, and kneel together, to worship God, revealed in a tiny child.

The next carol is based on Caribbean rhythms and reminds us of the richness of the gift that God gives us in Christ – from his poverty we have a wealth of love and grace. As we remember these gifts, the offering will be taken during the singing of this carol.

CAROL – SEE HIM LYING ON A BED OF STRAW

Prayers of Intercession
We have been reminded that God so loved the whole world that the Son was sent to be a Saviour for all, so now we pray for all in the world that God still loves.

"Loving God,
 Hear our prayers for your world."

Loving God,
We pray for the world you love
and all in it who are in need.

You came as a child, vulnerable and fragile, to share in our human life.
So we pray for the children of the world,
those in warm, comfortable homes, looking forward to Christmas,
and those living in fear of violence, war or famine, unsure how long they can survive.
Help us to cherish every child, and to lead them into your love.

Loving God,
Hear our prayers for your world.

You come as the Wonderful Counsellor to guide your people.
So we pray for those in need of guidance,
those who are struggling with their faith, or who have lost it altogether,
and those who are struggling with addiction, or loneliness, or illness.
Help us to listen to your guiding voice, and to share your words of comfort with those in need.

Loving God,
Hear our prayers for your world.

You come to your world as Mighty God,
so we pray for those who believe that strength is in violence and war,
and for those who suffer the consequences of that view.
And we pray for leaders who care only about political power rather than serving the people they lead.
Help us to challenge injustice and to work for peace.

Loving God,
Hear our prayers for your world.

You come to your world as the Eternal Father, caring for the weak and
 the lost,
so we pray for those who are homeless, living in doorways, or in
 carboard boxes,

and for the charities who work with them to provide shelter and warm
food.
Help us to be unselfish and make us aware of those in need of our help.

Loving God,
Hear our prayers for your world.

You come to your world as the Prince of Peace,
so we pray for those who live in fear of violence and oppression
and for those whose lives are chaotic and difficult because of choices
they, or their families, have made.
Help us to listen to their concerns, and to be a place of safety for them.

Loving God,
Hear our prayers for your world.

For a child has been born to us,
A son is given to us;
The government will be on his shoulders,
and his title will be:
Wonderful Counsellor, *Mighty God,*
Eternal Father, *Prince of Peace.*
In his name we offer our prayers, **AMEN**

The Lord's Prayer

The words of our next carol remind us that Christmas is about giving,
not only God giving himself to us, but us giving our hearts and lives to
others and to God. It was written by Christina Rossetti, and she was of
Italian extraction. The music was written by Gustav Holst, whose
mother was Spanish, and his father's family were Swedish, although he
also spent time in Russia and Germany. So they both seem to fit well
into the theme of "Joy to the World". Actually Gustav was born in
Cheltenham in the Cotswolds and is classed as an English composer, just
as Christina Rossetti is classed as an English poet because she was born
and brought up in London.

CAROL - IN THE BLEAK MIDWINTER

(the offering can be taken during this carol)

The Simple Things
Rossetti started with the simple things
the world around her
the earth as hard as iron
and water like a stone.

And then her imagination took flight
and she sees the stable
and the choirs of heaven
worshipping the child
whom heaven could not hold.

And she imagines
what comforted him
in the coldness of the stable -
being cradled in gentle arms
and nourished in love –
and asks if it was enough for God
why is it not enough for us?

We search for gifts
complex, expensive gifts
and overlook
the comfort of gentleness
and the nourishment of love
which cannot be gift-wrapped
except in humanity
and humility.

What can we give?
Our hearts, hands,
and time
to nourish with gentleness
and love.

John 1: 1-5, 14

The words of our final carol, written by Isaac Watts, sum up the message of our journey through the carols – that Christ came to the ordinary people and for the whole world.

CAROL – JOY TO THE WORLD

Benediction
May the peace of which the angels sang,
the joy that filled the shepherds
and the love that flows from the manger
fill our hearts, minds and lives
this Christmas time and for evermore. **AMEN**

Light Shining in the Darkness

This service was written in 2017. It had felt like a particularly difficult year as there had been terrorist attacks in Manchester and London; the Grenfell Tower disaster; the continuing refugee crisis; and escalating tension between the leaders of two nations with nuclear weapons. The aim of the service was to face these tragedies and recognise that within the darkness the light still shines, and that must give us hope. The news events could be changed to those that are more current if desired. The challenge then would be to find the light that shone in a different darkness.

PRACTICALITIES

The service works particularly well with two voices, one as the newsreader and the other as the leader, who also leads the prayers and introduces the carols and readings. Members of the congregation can be invited to read the lessons and meditations. It is probably a good idea to tell the congregation at the beginning that there will be deliberate pauses during which they can reflect on what they have heard.

Film-clips of the news items, or audio recordings are particularly effective. If these are not possible, then the 'newsreader' could be positioned to one side of the worship area, perhaps behind a desk, and remain there throughout the service.

The Leader can light an Advent candle as they speak the words "The light of …. shines in the darkness" and light the central candle as the words are read from John 1.

Leader   _Newsreader_

Readings: _Matthew 1: 18-25_   _Meditations:_   _Joseph_
                  Luke 2: 1-7   _The Innkeeper_
                  Luke 2: 8-20   _The Shepherd_
                  Matthew 2: 1-13   _The Wise Man_
                  John 1: 1-14

LIGHT SHINING IN THE DARKNESS

Call to Worship – Isaiah 9:2, 6

CAROL – O COME ALL YE FAITHFUL

Introduction

The major theme that runs through Advent into Christmas is hope. It is a hope that was central to Jewish faith, a hope for a Messiah who would come from God to bring a better future. Isaiah describes the Messiah as "the Wonderful Counsellor and Prince of Peace", someone who will bring healing to a broken world and encourage us to live peacefully with God and one another. During Advent this hope for a Messiah is often described as light shining in the darkness.

As we think back over 2017, we may feel that the darkness of world is overpowering. There have been disasters and tragedies; terror attacks and crises of power between World Leaders. It seems that the darkness is deep indeed, and it would be easy to give up hope.

Yet as the prophets remind us, God does not forget his promises, nor does he give up when the darkness seems deep and impenetrable. In Zechariah's song of praise he celebrates the tender compassion of our God who brings "the dawn from on high". So let us celebrate the light that shines in our darkness, however deep and dark, and which the darkness will never overcome.

Opening Prayer
Eternal God,
You are the light of the world,
the light of love, peace and truth.
You shine as a beacon in our lives
giving us hope that the darkness will not overcome us.

We celebrate that you are God
that you come to us in love
that you leave us with peace
and that you guide us with truth.
May the light of your hope burn brightly in our lives
now and always, **AMEN**

CAROL - TELL OUT MY SOUL, THE GREATNESS OF THE LORD

News item (clip or reading) – Manchester Bombing
On the evening of May 22nd, the American singer Ariana Grande was in concert at the Manchester Arena that was packed with excited young people and children. As the concert came to an end, a bomb was detonated in the lobby. Twenty-two people were killed, the youngest a girl of eight, and more than one hundred were injured. Many more were traumatised and live with the after effects of a terror attack. During the summer, there were more terror attacks, in London, and in Europe, all of which have had a lasting and life-changing effect on those who were there.

Reading: Matthew 1: 18-25

Joseph
It was hard when Mary told me,
told me that she was going to have a baby
and that I wasn't the father.
I was so happy when we got engaged,
I felt so proud that she was going to be my wife.
When people pointed to us

and smiled to us as we walked through the streets
I walked taller,
because Mary was by my side.

And now,
they're still pointing,
still talking about us,
but they are gossiping,
sniping,
judging,
making assumptions
without listening to the facts.

I was angry,
I shouted at God
asked why he'd chosen my Mary,
what we'd done to deserve this.
My family told me to walk away
to give her up
forget I'd ever met her.
But I had made her a promise
I told her I would be with her
whatever happened.
And I don't give up,
I don't break my promises.
This baby will grow up
knowing what faithfulness means.

Pause

Newsreader: As the news of the bombing spread, taxi drivers drove
into the danger zone of central Manchester to take
home traumatised children and parents. They drove
hundreds of miles, free of charge.

Leader: *(lights an Advent candle)*
And the light of courage shines in the darkness, and the darkness has never overcome it.

CAROL – CRADLED IN A MANGER MEANLY

News item – Refugees

Although they no longer feature in news bulletins, thousands of refugees are still trying to get to Europe to escape war, torture or poverty. Despite the patrols in the Mediterranean, the Greek islands and the coast of Italy continue to receive hundreds of refugees during the summer months. Although the Jungle Camp in Calais that once housed over 8000 refugees   has been cleared, the Channel ports are still full of people desperate to find a better life, struggling to survive without a roof over their heads or food to eat, wondering if the risks they have taken to get there were worth it.

Reading: Luke 2: 1-7

Innkeeper
I couldn't leave them out in the cold,
even though there was no room.
I saw them come into my yard,
exhausted, uncertain,
desperate for somewhere to stay,
for an end to their journey.

As he leaned against the wall,
quietly asking for somewhere to stay,
I saw the worry in his face
and the fear in his eyes.
I looked at her.
She was slumped on the ground
her aching legs unable to carry her any further.
There were blisters on her feet,
and bruises of exhaustion under her eyes.

I wanted to help,
I wished I had a room,
somewhere safe for them.

I told him that there was nowhere left
that even our small room
had been rented out.
I said that the only ones who were safe tonight
were the animals
because no one would want to sleep in the outhouse.
He turned to go
was about to help her up,
go and ask at another overcrowded inn,
when I heard myself say:
"But the straw's clean,
  and at least you'll have a roof over your heads,
  and the beasts will keep you warm."

Then I was fetching blankets
and food
and making them comfortable.
No, I had to do something,
I couldn't leave them out in the cold.

Pause

Newsreader: Communities across Europe have welcomed refugees,
and many more have raised money to send clothing,
food and shelter to the refugee camps for people they
will never meet.

Leader: *(lights an Advent candle)*
And the light of compassion shines in the darkness, and
the darkness has never overcome it.

CAROL - SILENT NIGHT, HOLY NIGHT

News item – Grenfell Tower

In the early hours of 14th June, a flat in the Grenfell Tower block in West London caught fire. The blaze spread in minutes and soon the entire tower was engulfed in flame. Firefighters rushed to the scene from across London and beyond and did their best to rescue residents and dowse the flames. They worked throughout the night, returning to the building time and again to try to reach people trapped in the 24 storey building. Despite their heroic efforts, more than eighty people died, and all the residents of Grenfell Tower were left homeless and without any possessions. Since the fire, there have been discussions and recriminations about why the flames spread so quickly, why sprinkler systems did not work, and why nothing had been done to help the homeless residents.

Reading: Luke 2: 8-20

Shepherd
Normally people ignore me,
or cross the road to avoid me.
Children shout at me,
Adults threaten me
"Go back where you belong,
  We don't want your sort here."
You see, shepherds aren't allowed in town,
not during daylight hours.
I suppose we spoil the look of the place
or we smell of sheep,
or both.

So I'm used to being ignored,
left out,
the last to know
and the first to be blamed.

So that night,
that incredible night,
when we heard the angels
and decided to come to town
we thought it would be a trap
something to catch us out.

So we couldn't believe we were the first,
the first to see the child
promised by Isaiah.
We couldn't believe we were welcome,
that the mother didn't turn us away
or turn up her nose.
She just listened
and showed us the child.
That night,
that wonderful night,
we felt as if we mattered
because we felt included.

Pause

Newsreader: Grenfell Tower was in one of the poorer communities in London, often overlooked for redevelopment and ignored when they asked for help.

Yet since that dreadful night, people within and outside the community have started to speak up, and to make their voices heard, to let the people of that area know that they have value, that they matter.

Leader: *(lights an Advent candle)*
And the light of inclusion shines in the darkness and the darkness has never overcome it.

CAROL – IT CAME UPON A MIDNIGHT CLEAR

News Item – North Korea/US power games
In the late summer, the tension between North Korea and the United
States increased dramatically as the countries' leaders fell into a battle
of words and unequivocal ultimatums, unseen since the worst days of
the Cold War. Each threatened to use nuclear weapons if the other did
not back down, and neither Kim Jung Il or Donald Trump wanted to be
the first to give way or back down. It seemed that the world was on
the brink of a nuclear holocaust, with no hope of compromise or a
concession to a different point of view. It felt as if national pride
mattered more than the future of the world as neither leader could
see the futility of a nuclear war that could endanger all life on earth.

Reading Matthew 2: 1-13

Wise Man
We'd had a long journey,
a tiring journey,
we weren't really sure where we going
we weren't really sure what we'd find
or whether we'd know if we found it.

We took several wrong turns
through difficult towns
or over rough boulders or desert.
The worst wrong turn took us to Herod.
In a palace that dripped with wealth
And bristled with the might of an army
we found a cunning man,
drunk on his reputation
and achievement,
yet also desperate,
desperate to hold on to power
desperate to be the most important
desperate enough

to wipe out all opposition.
We were glad to leave
glad that the child we sought was not his
that his palace was not the home of the Messiah.

After we had found the child
we discussed what to do.
The safest way home
was through Jerusalem
but that meant meeting Herod
and betraying the child.

The only other way
was through the desert,
full of natural and human dangers.
It wasn't the easy way
but it was the only way.
However treacherous for us,
however much we struggled,
it was the only way.

We were not going to betray the child.
We were not going to lead him to his death.

Pause

Newsreader: Whilst two leaders postured for war, many others were brokering peace, refusing to give in to the bullies.

When acts of terror incited some to racial hatred, many others called for understanding, for compassion, for tolerance.

Leader: *(lights an Advent candle)*
And the light of perseverance shines in the darkness, and the darkness has never overcome it.

CAROL - IN THE BLEAK MID-WINTER

Leader:

There have been moments of deep darkness this year, both personally and globally, when we have doubted that the light will ever shine again. Yet Advent and Christmas teach us that hope in God is never unfounded. He will keep his promise, he is Immanuel, God with us, the light will shine. He will come as the Wonderful Counsellor to encourage us to be faithful to our promises; as the Mighty God who cannot do nothing when people are in need; as the Everlasting Father who includes even those that no one else wants; and as the Prince of Peace who brings down the mighty, and turns away the threat of war. Although the headlines have been about acts of terror, the continuing refugee crisis, the Grenfell Tower fire, the threat of nuclear war, the light of God has continued to shine in acts of courage, compassion, inclusion and perseverance.

The light of God, the hope of the world, will shine in the darkness, and the darkness will never overcome it.

CAROL – O LITTLE TOWN OF BETHLEHEM

Prayers of Intercession

"Light of God
Shine in our darkness"

In silence we hold before God the people who have been injured or bereaved by terrorist attacks this year, and give thanks for the people who have helped them;

Pause

Light of God
Shine in our darkness

In silence we hold before God people who are refugees, fleeing their homes because of fear and oppression, and give thanks for those who have made them welcome;

Pause

> Light of God
> **Shine in our darkness**

In silence we hold before God the people who were injured made homeless or bereaved by the fire in Grenfell Tower, and give thanks for those who worked to save them and are helping them to rebuild their lives;

Pause

> Light of God
> **Shine in our darkness**

In silence we hold before God the fear of nuclear war and the leaders who play on that fear, and give thanks for the people who have persuaded them that there is another way;

Pause

> Light of God
> **Shine in our darkness**

God of Light, shine into the darkness of our world, give us hope, and the strength to work so that your light is seen, even in the darkest places.

For your name's sake we pray **AMEN**

The Lord's Prayer

CAROL – LIKE A CANDLE FLAME

John 1: 1-14

Silence during which the Christ candle is lit

CAROL – HARK THE HERALD ANGELS SING

Benediction
May the light of Christ,
the light that shines in the darkness
that the darkness can never put out;
shine in our hearts,
through our lives
and into our world
this Christmastime and for ever more. **AMEN**

Nativity Canticles

CONTEXT
This service is particularly suitable for Year C of the Revised Common Lectionary with its focus on the Gospel of Luke. The aim of the service is to explore what Luke was trying to tell his readers about Jesus' ministry through the four great songs associated with his birth. It gives an opportunity to look at the Benedictus and Nunc Dimittis which are not often included in carol services, as well as exploring the faith and politics behind the more familiar canticles of Mary and the angels. Through these songs, Luke sets out his understanding of Jesus' vision of the new Kingdom, where the expectations of the world are overturned.

PRACTICALITIES
This is a reasonably simple service to organise as it does not require props or reorganisation of the worship area. The theme of "Songs of the Nativity" gives a good opportunity for choirs and/or singing groups to be involved, especially if they can offer musical arrangements of the canticles at the appropriate point in the service. If no choir is available, the gospel readings will need to be extended to include the canticles.

This service was prepared for two leaders, but if only one is available, the meditations will flow just as well with one voice as with two. The Angels' Song meditation can be read by the two leaders, or by others if there are enough volunteers.

PEOPLE REQUIRED
Leader 1   Leader 2

Readings:	*Luke 1: 26-45*	*Meditations:*	*Magnificat*
	Luke 2: 1-7		*Benedictus*
	Luke 2: 8-20		*The Angels' Song*
	Luke 2: 21-38		*(two voices)*
	John 1: 1-14		*Nunc Dimittis*

THE NATIVITY CANTICLES

Call to Worship: Micah 5: v2 & v4

CAROL – HARK! THE HERALD ANGELS SING

Opening Prayers
Eternal God,
You created singing and laughter,
joy and sorrow,
to enrich our human lives.
You created hope, light and new life,
to encourage us
to reach towards you.

But we know we have turned from your way
ignoring what you want for your creation.
Forgive us for being obsessed with possessions and prestige;
forgive us for being ready to compromise our faith and values;
forgive us for closing our eyes and ears to you.
Help us to remember that you gave us your Son
a baby, born to a human family,
to show us how to use your creation,
to live life in all its fullness.

Open our ears so that we can hear again the song of the angels,
and respond with hearts overflowing with everlasting hope.
Open our hearts to receive your Son again
so that our hearts can beat in time with yours
and love with your love.
For the sake of your kingdom, **AMEN**

Introduction

1: This carol service is based around four great songs of the church's tradition, the Magnificat, the Benedictus, the Gloria and the Nunc Dimittis, which are sung by Mary, Zechariah, the angels and Simeon respectively.

2: These songs are known as the Nativity Canticles and can all be found in the Gospel of Luke.

1: His gospel is the one which was most thoroughly researched and therefore contains the greatest amount of detail, particularly about Jesus' birth.

2: But he wasn't just looking to be accurate, he also wanted to use the story of Jesus' birth to introduce the main themes of his account of his ministry.

1: Luke's gospel tells the story of Jesus as the story of a revolution, turning the religious and political worlds on their heads.

2: So in Luke's version of the nativity story, there are three songs of praise, each of which tell of the way God has touched the lives of ordinary people – Zechariah, Mary and Simeon – and turned their lives upside down.

1: These people were so moved by their encounter with God that they sang about their vision of God's world.

2: As we hear Luke's account of the birth of Jesus, we shall reflect on each song and why we still need to sing it today.

Luke 1: 26 – 45 Annunciation and Visit to Elizabeth

CAROL – TELL OUT MY SOUL, THE GREATNESS OF THE LORD

The Magnificat – Turning the World Upside Down
In Mary's situation, even today, would we feel like singing a song of praise to God? An unplanned pregnancy, a fiancé uncertain about

whether he wanted to get married, and a long tiring journey into the hills to visit a relative of her mother's.

Yet the first thing she does is to praise God for everything he has already done, and for not abandoning even the most insignificant of people, and counts her pregnancy as a blessing. Then she goes on to sing about the power of God to turn the world upside down. In the wonderful contemporary paraphrase we have just sung, it talks about "Powers and dominions" laying "their glory by" and "Proud hearts and stubborn wills" being "put to flight".

How much misery could be ended if proud hearts and stubborn wills were broken today, if powers and dominions were prepared to lay their glory by? And Mary is right, when we stop focussing on ourselves and our needs and keeping up with the neighbours, then the hungry can be fed, and the "humble, lifted high" because God has created enough for us all, if we could only learn how to share.

Luke is the only gospel writer who takes notice of a young girl from an ordinary family, chosen by God to do extraordinary things. And Mary isn't the only one, throughout Luke's gospel we meet ordinary people whose lives are turned upside down by their encounter with Jesus, who become part of his revolutionary new Kingdom of Love, forgiveness and peace.

Mary's song is revolutionary, turning the world on its head because it is concerned not with glorifying the rich and famous, but with celebrating the life and ministry of ordinary people. In fact, Mary's song of praise sets the agenda for Jesus' ministry, because it is about turning the world upside down, changing the way we see things, putting God first, and social status and standing at the bottom of the list.

Luke 1: 57-67 - The Birth of John the Baptist

Choir - Benedictus

The Benedictus – Freedom

What would you want to say if you have been silent for nine months? How much frustration or enthusiasm would be stored up and needing to be let out? Maybe some of us wish that that could happen to those with whom we live, so that they would no longer be able to nag at us, or distract us when we are doing something more important than listening to them! Zechariah was struck dumb as a punishment for not believing that God could fulfil his promises, and the first thing he does when he recovers his speech is not to rant at his wife about all the things she has been saying, or tell his neighbours all the gossip he has heard, but, like Mary, to sing a song of praise to God. Zechariah's song is about freedom from oppression, and the approach of God's salvation and forgiveness, for everyone. It echoes what the angel said to Mary "Nothing is impossible for God." So Zechariah sings of God's strength, and how he keeps his promises, and then in the most beautiful words he talks about "the tender compassion of God" and the dawn of heaven bringing light and salvation. This promise of light and forgiveness in a difficult world is what gives us hope that evil and despair has not and will not win, because God has promised us salvation, and God keeps his promises. And if we think that we are not important enough for God, then remember that for if God can come to ordinary people like Mary, Elizabeth and Zechariah, he can come to us in tender compassion and give us hope and salvation, and freedom from guilt, so that we too can sing praise with glad hearts.

CAROL – SILENT NIGHT, HOLY NIGHT

Luke 2: 1-7 – The Birth of Jesus

CAROL – WHILE SHEPHERDS WATCHED THEIR FLOCKS or *Choir: Gloria*

Luke 2: 8-20 – The Visit of the Shepherds

The Angels' Song (Two voices)

A: Can you imagine what it must have been like for the shepherds out on the hillside, looking out for nothing more startling than wolves and bears?

B: Suddenly they are flooded with light and something like the largest Hallelujah Chorus in the world suddenly starts up!

A: But more that that. The angels are singing praise to God and promising Peace on Earth.

B: Peace must have seemed like an impossible dream because the shepherds were living in a country occupied by the Romans.

A: Everyone was treated with suspicion and there were frequent acts of terrorism and violence against the Romans and against the Jews.

B: So the angels' song 'Glory to God in the highest, and on earth, peace to all people' would have been as shocking as the method of delivery was frightening.

A: We've got so used to this message, that over the years it has lost its power to surprise us.

B: But when the shepherds first heard it, they would have been amazed and afraid because it was a direct challenge to the authority of Rome and the Romans.

A: This was because the angels praised God, and not Caesar. If any Romans had heard it, there would have been arrests and punishment.

B: But the angels didn't stop there. They said that God is the source of all peace and goodwill, which would have upset the authorities even more because they believed that the Roman Empire brought peace and goodwill, not God.

A: No wonder the shepherds hurried off to Bethlehem to see what this infant revolutionary was like. He was going to overthrow the strongest political power the world had ever known.

B: So the angels' song is still revolutionary, still proclaims that God is greater than any other power, even money or nuclear weapons.

A: And the revolution continues, in ordinary people, like the shepherds, like us,

B: who believe in the extraordinary power of God.

CAROL – ANGELS FROM THE REALMS OF GLORY

Luke 2: 21-38 Anna and Simeon

Nunc Dimittis – Promises fulfilled
How many of us would have had the patience that Anna and Simeon showed?
Would we be prepared to wait so many years before God's promise was fulfilled?

Impatience seems to be everywhere these days, whether it's road rage, or having to queue for more than 30 seconds at the tills, we all seem to want things NOW rather than waiting. Yet Simeon and Anna trusted that God would fulfil his promise to them, and that they would see his salvation in their lifetime.

Would we have continued to go to the temple everyday?
Would we still have had that anticipation that today might just be the
        day?

Or would we have given up, saying that it was never going to happen,

Or given in to the taunts of our friends who kept telling us it was a waste
        of time?

Yet Anna and Simeon, like Mary, Zechariah and the angels, trusted in God, believed that he is a God who keeps his promises. They looked back at the way God had kept his promises to Israel in the past, rescuing them from slavery, guiding them to the Promised Land, bringing them back from Exile, and knew that God's promises can be trusted.

If we follow their example, then we can read of God's promises of salvation, light, hope, freedom from guilt and oppression, and know that we can trust God to deliver them, just as Anna and Simeon did. It's just that we also have to learn to trust in God's time, rather than expect God to work to our agenda.

In this frenetic world, we need to learn patience and trust, that God will act at the right time to fulfil the promise of salvation.

CAROL – BRIGHTEST AND BEST OF THE SONS OF THE MORNING

Singing our Own Song   *(Leader)*

1:      So those are the four nativity canticles. We usually hear the Magnificat and the Gloria when we read the Christmas story, but we rarely hear Zechariah's Benedictus or Simeon's Nunc Dimittis. But they are all part of the story because they share common themes. God turns the expectations of the world upside down, focussing not on power but on love; he comes to ordinary people, to bring them the light of salvation. Or to put it another way, he comes to give them hope of escape from the difficulties and problems that make life hard to bear, whether those difficulties are facing illness in ourselves or in those we love; or the worry and stress of debt; or a change in circumstances which mean that we have to give up cherished dreams or ways of life; or the difficulty of living in an impossible situation where you can see no way out, or are overwhelmed with memories of past problems. Each of the nativity canticles talks about shining light into the darkness, the light of salvation, the light of God's glory. He does this, not by removing the difficulties, but by bringing a different perspective, by changing priorities. He turns our expectations upside down showing forgiveness and love where we expect condemnation, and

133

tolerance and understanding where others shout for retribution. He does it by casting aside power and becoming a vulnerable child, coming not in glory, but in poverty.

2:     So what song would we sing if we were part of the Christmas story? Would we be singing the Magnificat, proclaiming a change of lifestyle? Or shouting aloud the Benedictus, that God is a God of tender compassion, who comes close to deliver his people from darkness; or would we be singing with the angels that peace on earth *is* possible when power and oppression are laid aside? Or are we patiently waiting, like Anna and Simeon, waiting to sing a song of completion, of promises fulfilled? Each song is a song of hope, or possibility, of a God who achieves the impossible by doing the outrageous and unthinkable. Each song is about daring to believe that God is with us, that each of us matters to God, no matter how insignificant we feel. That is why God brings light to the world, because he also brings hope, and that gives us the strength to carry on even when we do not feel like singing. So what song do you need to hear in your darkness, and what song will you be singing this year to shine God's light of love into our world?

CAROL – IT CAME UPON THE MIDNIGHT CLEAR

Prayers of Intercession

1:     To the bidding   "God of life: give us the strength"
please respond   **"To sing your song of love come down"**

To those whose lives have been turned upside down by unexpected news and events:

> God of life: give us the strength
> **To sing your song of love come down.**

2:      To those who are unable to speak because they are afraid, because they lack understanding or have been silenced by illness:

> God of life: give us the strength
> **To sing your song of love come down.**

1:      To those who long for peace on earth, living in the shadow of war, terrorism and oppression:

> God of life: give us the strength
> **To sing your song of love come down.**

2:      To those who are patiently waiting for healing, for understanding and for promises to be fulfilled:

> God of life: give us the strength
> **To sing your song of love come down.**

For the sake of your Kingdom we pray. **AMEN**

The Lord's Prayer

Offering (Choir – Like a candle flame)

CAROL – JOY TO THE WORLD

Benediction

1:      Everlasting God,
2:      open our hearts to feel your love,
1:      our ears to hear your song,
2:      and our lips to sing it to the world,
        this Christmastime and for evermore,
        AMEN

The Hardest Gift

CONTEXT
This service was more of a challenge than usual because the congregation were asked to choose favourite carols and explain why they liked them. Their choices and the reasons for the choice were woven into the service. Despite these choices being particular to that congregation, the explanations have been left in to show how choices can be woven into this style of service. Another thread to be included was the centenary commemoration of the Christmas Truce of 1914, the first Christmas of the Great War. This was done with a short film which concluded with "Silent Night" sung in German.

PRACTICALITIES
Each meditation has a prop associated with it. The reader of the meditation brings the prop to the front with them, and puts it on a table at the front to make a display. At the end of each meditation there is a pause, followed by a prayer which can be said by the reader of the meditation or by the leader of the worship.

PEOPLE AND PROPS REQUIRED

Leader	Readings:	Micah 5: 2-5a
		Luke 2: 1-7
		Luke 2: 8-20
		Matthew 2: 1-12
		John 1: 1-18

Meditation	Prop
The Promised Gift	Teddy Bear
For Family and Friends	Lists
The Unexpected Gift	Wrapped bottle
For Colleagues at Work	Label for a present

THE HARDEST GIFT

Call to Worship
We have come, as the faithful of all ages have gathered,
to hear again the story of the birth of the saviour,
to draw near to Christ's cradle
and to share in the choirs of angels.
We have come to worship and adore the True God and Light of all,
who comes to us in humility and love.

CAROL - O COME ALL YE FAITHFUL (NOT FINAL VERSE)

Introduction – What is the hardest gift to buy?
There are two inspirations for the carol service this year – firstly, an article written for the Circuit magazine on people's favourite carols, all of which are being sung tonight. So all the carols have been selected by members of the congregation, which could be a cunning way of me saying, if we aren't singing your favourite, don't blame me, blame everyone else for not picking it. The introit was two verses from "King Jesus had a garden", chosen by a member of the choir who finds that the words speak to her because of her love of gardening, and 'O Come All ye Faithful' was chosen by someone else who says that it is a carol they have known all their life, and for them it sums up the story of Christmas.

And the second inspiration has come from the television. According to advertisers, Christmas is a time when we think about gifts, especially those we need to purchase to give to other people, and apparently the more we spend on them, the more they will love us.

One particular advert caught my eye this year. I can't remember which company had commissioned it, so clearly it failed in its purpose, but there were several models and celebrities talking about the person for whom it is most difficult to buy a gift. As someone who does NOT like shopping, and especially does not like Christmas shopping, for me the answer was easy, everyone. But it did set me thinking, for whom do we find it hardest to buy gifts? Is it our family – or are we super-organised with lists? Is it friends, or work colleagues? And how do we judge how much or how little to give?

And what is our response to the gifts we receive, those we expect and those that are unexpected, the surprises that open our eyes to new ideas or a deeper understanding of our friendships? To help us explore these ideas, each Bible reading will be followed by a meditation, giving different perspectives on how people feel about giving and receiving gifts. At the end of each meditation there will be a brief time of silence, which will conclude with a prayer.

So as we reflect on gifts given and received, let us open our hearts to God in prayer, giving thanks for the gifts he gives us.

Opening Prayers based O Come all ye Faithful
Let us pray,
Gracious God,
We have come, joyfully and gladly to worship you,
to celebrate your amazing gift of love
when your Son, the King of the angels,
came to share our human life.
We have come to worship and adore you.

Living Saviour,
We have come, taking time out of our busyness,
to hear again the amazing story of your birth,
the God of God,
and Light of Light, who took on human form
so that we could really know
what God's love means,
making God's Word real in our lives.
We have come to worship and adore you.

Creative Spirit,
We have come, hopefully and expectantly,
to be reminded of your work
creating hope for ordinary people
changing lives and releasing potential
so that all people may reflect the glory of God.
We have come to worship and adore you.

Almighty God, Creator, Redeemer and Sustainer,
We offer you our hearts and lives
to be filled with your love and hope
as we worship and adore you,
In Jesus' name, **AMEN**

Our next carol was chosen because it seems that Christina Rossetti, the writer, explains the real meaning of Christmas, in one short phrase "Love came down at Christmas".

CAROL – LOVE CAME DOWN AT CHRISTMAS *(seated)*

Micah 5: 2-5a

The Promised Gift   *Prop – Teddy Bear*
I remember Christmas as a child.
I always knew what I was getting.
£1 from Uncle Fred,
knitted socks from Aunt Ruth,
chocolate from my cousins,
and something from my parents
for which I'd longed all year.

I remember the year I got teddy,
I'd looked at him in the shop window
every day on the way home from school.
His fur golden and soft,
his eyes brown and warm and shiny,
and he seemed to say
"Take me home and love me."

And every day,
my mother would gently pull me away
and say "Wait until Christmas."
And I would gaze back at teddy
and tell him that soon,
soon he'd be mine.

And that Christmas morning
when I opened the parcel
and there was teddy in his box,
just as I knew he would be.
I was so pleased,
I didn't let him out of my sight
for days afterwards.
I've cuddled him so much,
his fur's worn away,
and his eyes have gone dull,
but I can't throw him away.
He reminds me,
of how much I was loved
and of a mother and father
who always kept their promises.

Pause

Leader Loving God,
We thank you that you always keep your promises,
of forgiveness and renewal.
We pray for those people
who will not get any gifts this Christmas,
for the lonely, the bereaved, the homeless.
May they know your love surrounding and comforting
them.
In Jesus' name. **AMEN**

The next carol that was chosen because it has always been a family favourite for the chooser, who remembers their grandfather singing it when they were a small child. The choir will sing for us now, the Coventry Carol.

Luke 2: 1-7

For Family and Friends   *Prop – Lists*
I've been buying presents for the family
And it's not easy.
Young children get so many toys,
what can I get that's different?
I don't understand teenagers,
how they think or what they want.
And as soon as I do understand it,
they don't want it,
"That's so *last* year."
And as for the grown-ups,
they're the worst.
"We don't want much"
but are bitterly disappointed
if I believe them.

I could stick to vouchers
but I feel like a cheapskate,
Or if I resort to smellies,
that's the ultimate cop-out.
Whatever happened to
"It's the thought that counts"?
I think ever such loving thoughts
but they don't seem to appreciate it.

Last year,
I really thought they'd love what I'd bought them
but it's been gathering dust in a cupboard
since Boxing Day.

I do love my family,
I just wish they were easier to buy for,
more easily satisfied
with the simple things in life.

Pause

Leader Loving God,
We pray for those who have difficult family lives,
and for whom Christmas is especially traumatic.
As we give and receive presents,
help us to appreciate the loving thoughts behind every
gift.
For Jesus' sake, **AMEN**

Our next carol was chosen because, for one lady, the words immediately create a sense of happiness in a humble stable, yet there are words in the last verse that can make us feel sad. It says 'who have winter but no Christmas bringing them thy peace on earth'.

CAROL – CRADLED IN A MANGER MEANLY

Luke 2: 8-20

The Unexpected Gift   *Prop – Wrapped bottle*
My neighbour's given me a present,
she doesn't usually.
It's a really nice surprise,
but I feel ever so embarrassed.
I haven't got her a present,
and I wouldn't know what to get her.

I don't know why she's done it,
I've not spoken to her this year
any more than I did last,
and suddenly she's given me a present.
I haven't unwrapped it,
do you think I should?

It might help me to know
how much to spend on her!

But why should I buy her something
just because she's bought something for me?
Maybe that's why she's bought it,
so that I'll buy something for her.

But what if it's not a nice gift,
what if it's some weed-killer
and she's dropping hints
about the state of the garden?
It's shaped like a bottle,
so it could be.

I really don't know what to do,
I don't like unexpected gifts,
It throws out all my plans,
and I have to start all over again.

Pause

Leader: Loving God,
Help us to appreciate the unexpected gifts,
the small things that let us know
that we are loved and valued.
And help us to find ways to show others
that we love and value them.
For Jesus' sake, **AMEN**

Our next carol was chosen because it brings back memories of Christmas past for one lady. She especially remembers trudging through thick mud to sing this at outlying farms.

But this year, as we commemorate the centenary of the outbreak of the First World War, it also recalls the unexpected gift of peace on Christmas Day, 1914, when soldiers voluntarily laid down their weapons to share in celebrating the birth of Christ. It was the famous Christmas Day truce, a spontaneous outbreak of peace in the midst of war.

Cue "This short film illustrates the truce."

The Christmas Truce (Film)

Silence

Cue for organist: As we think of all those who have fought for the cause of freedom, and are still caught up in fighting and violence, we remain seated and sing "Silent Night"

CAROL – SILENT NIGHT *(seated)*

Matthew 2: 1-12

For Colleagues at Work   *Prop – Label for a present*
Someone in the office
has suggested that this year
we do "Secret Santa".
We've all got to buy a present
for the person we've been allocated
on our label.
It's supposed to help us cut costs
and make Christmas less embarrassing
for those who don't get lots of presents.

I suppose it does help
because we don't have to buy for people
we don't really like
and we don't have to pretend
that what they buy us
is what we've always wanted.

And then there's the problem
of what to buy the boss.
If we spend too much
we look like we're crawling,

if we don't spend enough
do we risk being overlooked
next time there's a promotion?

Personally
I'd rather give money to charity
than give presents at work.
But if I say that,
I'll look sanctimonious
or be told "You're missing the point."
But Secret Santa?
Is that really the answer?
Isn't it missing the point
of giving gifts to show love
and appreciation,
and valuing the individual?
Or am I just in a bad mood
because I don't know what to get
for Janice in Accounts?

Pause

Leader   Loving God,
We thank you for people who work at Christmas
to ensure our safety, our warmth, our happiness.
We pray for those who are unemployed,
who struggle to know how to support themselves or their
     families.
May they know that they are valued,
and may they have your peace this Christmas.
For Jesus' sake, **AMEN**

Our next carol has been chosen because of its associations with working
with young people in Whitby in 1975. We stand to sing:

CAROL – BORN IN THE NIGHT

For your Beloved   *(Leader)*

It's very hard to find a gift
for the one you love.
It's supposed to sum up
all they mean to you
and all your understanding of them.
Some years you spend ages
listening for subtle hints
or looking for their favourite authors.
And other years,
you give up in despair
and go for something funny
to cover your lack of inspiration.

And I'm told
it's so much harder for men
because they can't understand
why women don't want
kitchen utensils
or a new vacuum cleaner
for Christmas.

So what do we give our beloved?

God loved humankind
and gave us creation,
a place in which to grow and thrive.
But we couldn't agree how to use it
and fell out with one another.

He promised gifts
of freedom and equality,
but we set them aside
for selfishness and easy gain.

He sent prophets and priests
to show its potential
to reveal the unexpected gifts,
but we ignored them as do-gooders.

He sent punishment in flood
and exile
but we soon forgot him.

But despite our rejections
God does not give up on us.

God keeps his promises,
He sent his son, Jesus Christ,
an unexpected, undeserved gift of love.
To show us how to give and receive
to lead us back to fullness of life.
And in giving himself for us
to reveal how much we mean to God,
each and everyone
beloved and valued
as his precious child.

John 1: 1-18

The next carol is one that brings back memories of nativity plays. Each year the schoolchildren had to learn the final verse of this carol by heart, so that they could sing it unaccompanied. And that particular verse poses the question, at this time of giving gifts, what are we giving to God who loves us so much?

CAROL – IN THE BLEAK MID-WINTER

We hear a carol chosen by one of our instrumentalists because she has just learned to play it on the oboe, so she will play it for us now as we take up our offering.

Offering – *Ensemble – Good King Wenceslas*

Collect
God of Love and Light,
of gifts and giving:
open our eyes to your grace
and our hearts to your love,
so that we may respond with joy
to the gifts of Christmas;
through Jesus Christ our Lord, **AMEN**

The Lord's Prayer

Our final carol was chosen by one of the young people, because it goes fast and is lively. So we take a deep breath and stand to sing:

CAROL - DING DONG MERRILY ON HIGH

Benediction
May God fill us with joy, hope, peace and humility this Christmas, that our lives and our gifts may reflect his love and forgiveness. And may his blessing, the blessing of the Father, Son and Holy Spirit, be upon us, now and always. **AMEN**

With the Poor – A Dalit Candlelight Service

CONTEXT

Dalits are the lowest caste in Indian society, often known as "The Untouchables". They do many of the dirty jobs such as street cleaning and working amongst the sewage because no one else will do it. Dalits are often forced to eat from clay pots as a symbol of their low social stature. The pots are then smashed to ensure that no one of any other caste uses it and is contaminated by the Dalits' caste or the dirty jobs they do. This only underlines to the Dalits how unwanted they are.

This service starts with the story of the Dalits and the oppression they endure, and moves on to ask the question "Who are the Untouchables, the excluded in our society?" Using characters from the original Christmas story, the congregation are prompted to reflect on the message of Christmas to each excluded group. Each meditation concludes with the lighting of a Dalit candle and a prayer. If the church has AV capability, projecting the image of the "Dalit Madonna" from the Methodist Collection of Modern Art would add greater emphasis to the message of God coming to outsiders.

PRACTICALITIES

The Dalit Candles are available online (www.dalit.co.uk) and from Fair Trade sources such as Traidcraft and the Ethical Superstore. Copies of the Dalit Madonna image are available from Methodist Publishing.

Each meditation ends with a prayer, which is said by the leader of worship as they light a candle. If Dalit candles are used, there should be four smaller candles arranged around one large one, as in an Advent ring. One smaller candle is lit after each of the first four meditations. The large central candle is lit at the appropriate point in the final mediation, which is read by the leader.

There is no distinct part of the service for prayers of intercession as the prayers that conclude each meditation are intercessory. These should be taken at a measured pace, with appropriate pauses.

In Elizabeth's meditation, the final lines of each stanza that are in quotation marks could be read in a sarcastic voice, perhaps mimicking those who have excluded her.

PEOPLE NEEDED

Readings: Luke 1: 38-45   *Meditations:*   Elizabeth
                Luke 2: 1-7   Joseph
                Luke 2: 8-20   The Shepherd
                Matthew 2: 1-13   The Servant
                John 1: 1-14

WITH THE POOR

Call to Worship
Come, listen,
hear the story of God
coming down from heaven to earth
to shelter in a stable
and bring salvation to all people.

CAROL - ONCE IN ROYAL DAVID'S CITY

Introduction
We are here to celebrate the birth of Christ, by singing familiar and new carols and listening to the story of God coming to earth to share our human life. During Advent we have lit candles to remind us of the coming of the light of God in Jesus Christ. Tonight we will light these candles made by the Untouchable Caste in India as a reminder that Jesus came to the needy, poor and lowly. The Untouchable, or Dalit caste are the poorest group in Indian society. They perform dirty jobs, clearing

rubbish, working in the sewers and amongst animals which, according to religious tradition, makes them untouchable. Members of other castes are forbidden to associate with Dalits and they are excluded from participating in any social events or religious meetings. We light these candles as a prayer for those who are excluded, praying that they will know inclusion and welcome in Jesus' name.

Opening Prayer
Eternal God,
You came down to earth from heaven
Stepping into history,
into our time and space
to show us your unending love.
Tonight, we remember that you came in poverty
to show that you do not value wealth;
that you came as a child
to show that you do not value strength.
that you came to a borrowed stable
to show that you do not value status or power.

We worship you for your vulnerable love;
for the challenge you offer to selfishness and pride;
and for your willingness to shine light into the darkest places.

May we, like the star that shone above Bethlehem,
reflect the light of your love and guide others to your cradle.
For your name's sake. **AMEN**

Dalit Candles
How are you going to dress your dining table this Christmas? Have you bought special serviettes or even splashed out on a tablecloth with Christmas motifs? Have you got special table decorations, perhaps even angel chimes that have served faithfully for many years? Do you indulge in Christmas crackers or do you hate the hats or jokes? Whatever you have got planned for the table, at this time of year almost everyone gets out their best crockery, possibly family heirlooms that are made from

fine bone china that have been kept carefully in a cupboard since last Christmas, and then cleaned ready to be used this year.

But how would you feel if you were served and had to eat from clay, unglazed and unfired? Because that is all that the Dalits are allowed to use, clay plates, pots and vessels made from the earth and dried in the heat of the sun. It is a sign of their exclusion and the low esteem in which they are held. And to add insult to injury, the pots are then broken to make sure that they cannot contaminate anyone else with the Dalits' untouchability. That is why these Dalit candles are made in clay pots, using a symbol of the means of their oppression to bring them light and hope. Through our purchase and use of the candles they are given a way out of the oppression of poverty. Each candle we light is a prayer that barriers that exclude will be broken down and that those who are oppressed will be set free. As we hear the familiar stories, listen to the meditations, and light these candles, we are encouraged not only to think of those across the world who are excluded, but also those in our own lives and society who are left out because they are different or because they challenge our way of thinking.

CAROL – THE ANGEL GABRIEL FROM HEAVEN CAME

Luke 1: 38-45

Elizabeth
I'm Elizabeth,
wife of Zechariah,
cousin of Mary.
And since I've been a married woman,
I've been excluded,
because I am different.
I wasn't what people expected
of a young wife,
didn't conform to what was wanted
didn't do my duty.

My body, this clay pot,
hasn't done what was expected
won't respond in the same way as others,
I haven't produced children
for my husband and his family.
So I am treated with pity
and as a freak.

I am excluded
from conversations about babies
and feeding, and teething
and nappies,
"Because you don't know what it's like"

I am excluded
from get togethers
to share the newness of motherhood
"because you wouldn't understand".

I am excluded
from gatherings of mothers
waiting for the end of the school day
"because you don't know how lucky you are"
as if *I* have chosen to be different.

I get strange looks
for trying to join in
for trying to understand.
I get pity
"for my pathetic attempts to belong."

It's not my fault,
It's the way I am made.

No one sees the light of faith
burning in this clay jar,
no one cares

that I care
that I am excluded.

But I am the clay pot
that God has chosen
to fill with light and hope.
I am the light of the dawn
of his tender compassion.

Pause

Leader: Elizabeth did not choose to be childless, any more than
             Dalits choose to be born into the untouchable class.
             It was the people who judged her who were at fault.

I light a candle for the Elizabeths of today:
the people we exclude because of the way they look,
or life choices they have made,
or that have been made for them.
God sees their light, where we see useless clay.

Loving God,
forgive our suspicions and prejudice
against those who are different from us.
Help us to see your light shining in them.
And through us,
Shine the light of your love into their lives.

CAROL – O LITTLE TOWN OF BETHLEHEM

Luke 2: 1-7

Joseph   *(Homeless)*
I'm Joseph,
of the house of David,
the royal family of Bethlehem.
At least,
I thought I was one of the family

154

that I'd be welcomed
and found a place
even at the busiest time.

I've tried to find where I belong
Searched for the people I thought I knew,
But I've been excluded
doors closed in my face
some of them slammed
others apologetically closed,
My dialect marks me out as different,
I don't belong here,
I'm from the North,
I don't matter.

Yes, my clothes are dusty with travel
covered with the clay of the road,
but so are many others.
I have been sleeping outside
under hedges and in barns
because the inns were full
and we were saving our money
for this town.

People I thought I knew
have turned me away.
Those to whom I thought I was close
have looked at me with distrust
and suspicion.
They looked at Mary
who is not yet my wife,
saw her "condition"
and frowned their disapproval.
They have closed their minds to us
as firmly as they have closed their doors.

They would not listen to our story
to the joy that is burning within us.
They judged us,
and turned us away,
not wanting to be tainted
by association with us.

The innkeeper is not family
but he is a compassionate man.
He took pity on us
and now we shelter with the animals
and eat from clay pots.
I pray that my son
will have more compassion
than my family.

Pause

Leader: Joseph did not choose to be homeless, any more than
              Dalits choose to live and work in the slums.
              It was not his fault,
              he was obeying the law and custom of the land.

I light a candle for the Josephs of today:
the people we exclude because we have no room for
          them:
the children who have fallen out with their parents, or
          step-parents;
the people with whom we have fallen out;
those who take too much time or effort to care for
those who challenge our thinking.
God sees their light, where we see worthless clay.

Loving God,
forgive our hard-heartedness
and our unwillingness to forget past hurts.

Help us to see your light shining in them.
And through us,
Shine the light of your love into their lives.

CAROL – CRADLED IN A MANGER MEANLY

Luke 2: 8-20

Shepherd   *(Carers)*
I'm a shepherd,
I work in the fields above Bethlehem.
I'm the dependable one,
the one who puts the sheep first,
so I'm always left behind,
always left out
when something happens.

When the angels had gone,
the others rushed off without looking back
saying "you don't mind staying"
"Keep an eye out for bears"
without even asking if I minded.

The night looked darker when I was alone
the howls of the wolves louder
and closer.
The fire burned low
compared with the light of the angels.
The cold, bare earth on which I sat
did not warm me.
It was unyielding
and unforgiving.

I checked on the sheep
they were asleep
oblivious to the cold and the dark
lost in their own world
where I cannot go.

I did not speak
there was no point
they would only have stared
unable to understand my words.

One stirred,
unsettled, uneasy,
I murmured meaningless words.
She gazed at me
unable to grasp my meaning
but comforted by my presence
and settled back to sleep.
The silence engulfed me
smothering me with the awareness
of being left behind again.

Distant echoes of the angels' song
still rang in my ears.
I wondered what was happening,
what the others were seeing,
what I was missing, again.

Hours later,
they came back as they always do,
bubbling over with excitement
telling me all about it
interrupting each other
in their haste to convey
the wonder and the glory they had seen.
"You should have been there" they gasped.

And then I snapped
as I have always wanted to
"I couldn't BE there.
Someone had to be HERE!
Someone had to care.

And one day
it won't be ME".

They shuffled their feet,
looked embarrassed
and then carried on talking
as if I hadn't spoken.
I just want someone to listen
to notice that I too have a light
burning inside this reliable old clay pot.

Pause

Leader: The shepherd did not choose to be left behind to tend
the sheep, any more than the Dalits choose to be left out
of social and religious events.
It was not his fault.
He was putting the needs of others first.

I light a candle for the shepherds of today:
the people we exclude because they have
responsibilities they cannot leave;
the people who care for members of their family;
those who feel that life is passing them by, and they are
forgotten.
God sees their light where we see only dependable
reliability.

Loving God,
Forgive our forgetfulness of the burden of care that
people carry.
Help us to see your light shining in them.
And through us,
Shine the light of your love into their lives.

CAROL – WHILE SHEPHERDS WATCHED

Matthew 2: 1-12

Servant of the Magi   *(The Unseen Workers)*

I'm a servant of the Magi.
I serve my master,
quietly, efficiently
unobtrusively.
I'm good enough
to clear away his rubbish
or wipe his fevered brow
and listen to his tortured dreams,
but I'm not good enough
to be welcomed as a friend
or treated as an equal.

I'm good enough
to serve his magnificent food,
onto extravagant gold dishes
and watch as he nibbles at it
and then throws it to the dogs.
But I'm not good enough
to eat with him
or from his dishes.
I eat from clay pots
the scraps that neither he,
nor the dogs, want.

I'm good enough
to advise him
on the latest fashion,
whether it flatters
and when to wear it,
but I'm only good enough
for a uniform
that hides who I am
and shows who owns me.

I cannot share his world,
I can only stand on the outside
looking in,
unthanked, unnoticed
just one more clay pot
of no value.

And now,
I'm good enough
to travel with them
on this strange journey,
good enough to take care of his gift
to guard it
and treasure it,
but not good enough
to offer it
to this strange King
born in a stable,
to a poor mother
and a carpenter father.

He'll eat from clay pots
as I do,
He'll live with ordinary people
as I do,
He'll work unthanked
and be taken for granted
as I am,
but he'll not be invisible.
He will show
that the light of God shines from clay pots
even more brightly
than from gold or silver,
and that even clay pots are valuable to God.

Pause

Leader: The servants of the Magi did not choose to be invisible or left out of the Christmas story any more than Dalits choose to live out of sight and untouched by others.
It was not their fault,
it was those who were too proud to admit that they could not manage without help.

I light a candle for the servants of today:
those whom we take for granted and never remember
    to thank;
those who do the dirty or difficult or dangerous jobs
    that we don't want to do;
those who do jobs that disrupt family time and take
    them away from home at Christmas.
God sees their light, when we see nothing at all.

Loving God,
forgive our thoughtlessness
and our deliberate blindness
towards those who do difficult and thankless jobs.
Help us to see your light shining in them.
And through us,
Shine the light of your love into their lives.

CAROL – LIKE A CANDLE FLAME

Leader: God cares
for the unwanted outsiders.
In Jesus Christ,
he came to be with
the poor, the meek, the lost, the unwanted,
those scarred, battered and bruised
by life on the edge.

God cares
for those who feel ignored.
In Jesus Christ
he lived on the edge of society,
tolerated
but not welcomed
by those in power
edged out of conversations
because his opinion
was difficult
and challenging.

God cares
for those who are frustrated.
In Jesus Christ
he was angry with oppressors
and those who exploited the poor
and the ill.
He was frustrated
by intolerance
and unwillingness to help.
He rebuked their fear
of difference
and welcomed
the leper and the lame.

God cares
for those on the edge of survival.
In Jesus Christ
he reached out to the beggars
ignored by indifferent passers-by
more intent on their own comfort
than the misery of others.

God cares
for those on the edge,
of life, of sanity, of survival.
In Jesus Christ,
he came to the edge.
He was born in an outhouse,
lived on other people's handouts,
was mocked for his views
but still spoke against cosy religion
and greedy self-interest.
He was persecuted
and crucified
for being different
for being on the edge
and loving and welcoming
those he found there.

God cares,
because in Jesus Christ
God has been there,
and is still there.

Light central candle

God is the light in the window
drawing us in
welcoming and enfolding us in love.

God is the light in the eyes
that encourages to trust
that we have worth.

God is the light of hope
that gives us strength
in the darkness of despair.

God is the light
that shines in and through
every clay jar
and the darkness will never overcome it.

John 1: 1-5

CAROL – HARK! THE HERALD ANGELS SING,

Benediction
May the light of God
that fights fear and prejudice
and warms our hearts with love
burn in us this Christmastide, and for evermore. **AMEN**

CHRISTMASTIDE and EPIPHANY

Looking Back, Looking Forwards

This service invites the congregation to look back over the last year and recognise where God has walked with them, and to look forward to the new year and consider the resolutions they want to make. It is designed to be conversational so that people can talk to one another. It could work well as a café style service. Consideration should be given to how each period of conversation is going to be brought to an end. It could be with music, or a given signal from the leader. There should also be provision for those who want to listen but not necessarily participate in the conversations.

Looking Back, Looking Forwards

Call to Worship
Come, let us worship God
for Jesus, whose birth we celebrate,
is the same yesterday, today and forever.

Christmas Day Advent Liturgy, all candles are lit.

Gathering – Looking Back
Have you noticed that social media are forever reminding us of what we were doing a year or two or three ago? And asking us to comment on what we have done since.

And now we're at that time of year when the television schedules are full of reviews of the last twelve months, so perhaps it's a good time of year for us to reflect on our lives.

So this service is going to be a little bit different, we'll think back to the resolutions made last year. Can anyone remember what they were? Or are they the same every year?

Is anyone prepared to reveal how many they have managed to keep? Was it easy or difficult?

Perhaps you don't make resolutions, you prefer to set targets or hopes for the year, does anyone want to say how many projects they started, or more importantly finished?

But whatever we have hoped or strived for, we have hope and reason to rejoice because God's purpose remains the same – to reveal how much we are loved and to bring grace and peace to the world.

CAROL – JOY TO THE WORLD

Prayer of Adoration
Eternal God,
We sing songs of joy
because your love has come into the world.

Jesus Christ,
We sing to welcome you
the light of God, coming into our darkness.

Living Spirit,
We sing to praise you
for the life-giving energy you bring.

Trinity of love,
we share with you our joy
that you come to this world, bringing hope and light.

May your great name be praised,
now and always, AMEN.

Psalm 147

Hearing the Angels' Song
During Advent we were encouraged to think about the kind of King we are expecting. The King who was born on Christmas Day confounded all the usual human expectations by being born to poor parents in an outhouse in a forgotten city.

In contrast to that lowliness, we have just heard the psalmist celebrate God as the King of all creation, the acknowledge ruler of the world. The psalmist rejoices at the joy of knowing God, and of living in the light of his love.

So, let's turn to those around us and have a conversation. If we think back over the year – when have we known joy of living in light of God's love?

Conversation

Over the Christmas period we may have sung *It came upon the midnight clear*. Perhaps you were struck again by the poignancy of the words "beneath the angel strain have rolled, 2000 years of wrong."

It's very easy to agree with the line that follows "And man at war with man hears not, the love song that they bring." But if we think about it, there have been instances of people hearing the angels' song of peace.

Let's turn to those nearby and share our ideas - thinking globally and locally – of where has the angel song been heard?

Conversation

Conclusion
We thank God that there are those who are prepared to take the risk of listening to the angels' song, and of sharing love and peace with one another.

CAROL – IT CAME UPON THE MIDNIGHT CLEAR

Ephesians 1: 3-14

God's Purpose for the World
This passage shows Paul setting out what Christ's life and death mean for us. And not just for those of us gathered here, but for the whole world. For Paul, it is about atonement – setting things right, with God and with one another. It's about hearing the angels' song and applying it to our lives.

The next question then, is obvious, what can I do to help others hear the angels' song? It's not one to which we can all give an instant answer. Perhaps it is one we don't want to answer in public.

So let's take a moment of quiet to think about the resolutions or commitments we are going to make at New Year. How many of them are resolutions to help others or to listen more closely to God?

SILENCE

Prayer of Confession

CAROL – LOVE CAME DOWN AT CHRISTMAS

Reflecting on the Commandments
During Advent, not only are we encouraged to think about the King we are expecting, the communion liturgy suggests that we read the commandments of Jesus each week. They should give us a clue about the type of King God will send,

> "You must love the Lord your God with all your heart, with all your strength, with all your mind and with all your soul, and you shall love your neighbour as yourself."

> "Love one another, just as I have loved you, you also should love one another."

From that we should notice that God is sending a King of Love, who comes to heal and comfort and encourage.

And that is what links the readings today – that Love came down at Christmas, the King of Love, sent by God to rule in our hearts.

As we approach a new year, our hope for [2017] is that love for God, for our neighbour and for one another will be uppermost in our minds.

We've already thought about how we can love others, so now it's time to think about our love for God. There's no need to answer this question, - how deep is your love for God, and how can it be deepened?

172

The quick answer is to spend more time in prayer and Bible study. But it's not always that easy. It is about attitude. Sometimes we do things to tick boxes – I am praying, I can tick that off the list, but something should be happening, why isn't it?

It's really a question of whether we dash through a liturgy in a prayer book or take time to reflect on the words we are saying. Sometimes even familiar words can be so overwhelming that we cannot say them.

But perhaps we have become too familiar with our prayer routine, and to come closer to God we need to pray in different ways, in a different place or with different people so that we can find new ways of hearing God.

Let's have a final conversation with those around us to share our ideas about where we feel closest to God and what helps us to pray.

Conversation

So, on what will we concentrate in the coming year?

The Word made flesh, the light of the world, dwelling amongst us, bringing hope and peace to all, and how we can celebrate that word so that others around us can also hear and be drawn into God's love.

I pray that it is.

CAROL – BRIGHTEST AND BEST OF THE SONS OF THE MORNING

Prayers of Intercession -Petitions for prayer may be invited from the congregation.

A possible conclusion to each petition is "Loving God, **Hear our prayer"**

The leader concludes with:
Ever-loving God,
you have understood our thoughts and heard our prayers.
Enfold those for whom we have prayed
in the strength of your love and peace,
now and always, AMEN

The Lord's Prayer

Offering
For your gift of love and grace
Eternal God, we thank you;
and we offer you our gifts,
to continue the work of your Kingdom
and shine your light of love into the world.
For Jesus' sake, AMEN

CAROL – HAIL TO THE LORD'S ANOINTED

Benediction
May the love of God inspire us,
the grace of Christ uphold us,
and the life of the Spirit encourage us;
and may God's blessing rest upon us all,
now and through the coming year AMEN

This is another service that is designed to be conversational. In this service, a Taizé chant In the Lord I'll be ever thankful *was played to signal that conversations should draw to a close.*

In the Methodist tradition, New Year is a time for renewing our commitment to God through the annual Covenant Service. The Covenant prayer was first used by John Wesley, who adapted it from a prayer that the Moravians used. It is a demanding prayer, asking us to put our whole lives at God's disposal, and saying that we will accept whatever God chooses to do with our lives.

This service includes the use of the hymn "And are we yet alive, to see each other's face?" which is traditionally sung at the opening of the annual Methodist Conference. It is appropriate to sing it in this season, however it is not particularly well-known, even in Methodist Churches, so an alternative may be preferred.

Preparing for New Year

Call to Worship
God is the beginning and the end,
the first and last of all time.
Let us praise God's holy name.

CAROL - O COME ALL YE FAITHFUL

Opening Prayers

Living God,
you are the God of every time and place
you are more infinite than space
and as close as our heartbeats,
you see vast horizons
and the most minute detail of the smallest creatures.

You are beyond our understanding,
but yet also within our hearts
and touching our lives.
We praise you,
we worship you,
even though we do not understand
because of the meaning you give to your lives
and the love you show to us
that gives us hope and new life.

Loving God,
We know that we have not shared the love that you offer
we have closed our eyes to the needs around us
and concerned ourselves only with what immediately affects us.
We are sorry,
for our selfishness,
our lack of concern,
our unwillingness to help others.

Forgive us,
and help us to know that we are forgiven,
for your name's sake. **AMEN**

Isaiah 63: 7-9

Reflecting on the Year
Isaiah says "I shall recount the Lord's unfailing love, and all he has done for us. If we were Isaiah, looking back on the last year, what would we say? If our lives could be shown as footprints in the snow, what would we see?

That's the theme for our service today, looking back over the last year and seeing where God has been with us. After all, it is the time of year for retrospectives in newspapers and on the television. So today we have time to think about what we have done, and what we have given and received this year in God's name. This can help us to prepare for the renewal of our Covenant in the coming weeks. Please feel free to either discuss things with those around you, sit quietly and reflect on your own. The Taizé chant *In the Lord I'll be ever thankful* will be played to signal when it is time to bring the conversations to a close.

So as we prepare to reflect on the last twelve months, we sing a hymn that is sung at the opening of Conference each year. The words are also appropriate as we move into a new calendar year.

HYMN – AND ARE WE YET ALIVE?

Things Learned
The first question is "what have we learned this year?"

Perhaps it's a new skill, or a new language. Maybe it's how to get on with one another, or how impatient and grumpy we are? Because we're never too old to learn, there's always something to see or new things to discover. So let's share with one another how learning has enriched our lives.

Conversation

Music

Prayer
Living God,
For the opportunities we have shared
for learning and growing,
for noticing and remembering,
and for discovering and understanding,
Living God,
We give you thanks and praise.

As we move into a new year
may we remain alert to new ideas
and ready to take up new challenges,
for your name's sake.
AMEN

CAROL – SEE AMID THE WINTER'S SNOW

Things experienced/People met
Let's move on from things we have learned to things we have experienced. Have you been somewhere new or had a new experience? Maybe you've travelled in a helicopter, or have got your first bus pass, or you've finally got to grips with Facebook?

And what about the people you have met, or with whom you have met up after a long time apart. Maybe you have actually got round to talking to the neighbour to whom you have been waving for weeks, or you remember the person who sat next to you on the bus.

So what have you done, and who have you met, and in whom have you seen light of Christ?

Conversation

Music

Prayer
For the new experiences we have had
for the people we have met
for the love we have discovered
Living God,
We give you thanks and praise.

As we move into a New Year
may we continue to share the love we have experienced
for your name's sake **AMEN**

CAROL - IN THE BLEAK MIDWINTER

Matthew 2: 13-23

Items in the News.
This passage from Matthew is not an easy passage to hear. We don't want the Christmas story to end with bloodshed and violence. But we have to face the reality that it does, just as we have to face the reality

178

that things happen in the world that are not good news. Let's talk to one another about what has been in the news this year, -wars, natural disasters, political manoeuvring.

Conversation

Music

Prayer
For being with us in the difficult times
for carrying us when we could no longer walk
for giving us hope that hatred and evil would not have the last word;
Living God,
We give you thanks and praise.

Be with those who are suffering now,
who are lonely,
who are frightened,
and enfold them in your everlasting arms
so that they may now strength and peace;
for your name's sake we pray. **AMEN**

CAROL – LOVE CAME DOWN AT CHRISTMAS

Incredible gift received
The carol talks about the love that came down at Christmas. So, let's think now of the gifts we have received, not just this Christmas, but throughout the year – the presents on special occasions, or the unexpected gifts.

And think also of the gifts we have received from God – friendship, peace, strength, courage, laughter and hope. How have they brought us through this year?

Conversation

Music

Prayer

For all the gifts we have had the opportunity to give,
and for all the gifts we have received,
the expected and the unexpected -
those that have brought laughter
and those that have brought strength;
Living God,
we give you thanks and praise.

And in this season of Christmas,
most of all we give you thanks and praise
for the Incredible gift of love you give to us
in your Son, Jesus Christ.
For his birth amongst ordinary people,
for his ministry of healing and teaching
for his death and resurrection
through which you give us new life and hope
We worship you
and we give you our thanks and praise
For his name's sake, **AMEN**

CAROL – LET EARTH AND HEAVEN COMBINE

Prayers of Intercession

With those with whom we have been talking, let us come together in prayer. You may want to mention people or situations for whom you would like to pray, or you may prefer to sit in silence, thinking over the last year.

Our time of prayer will conclude with the chant, after which we shall say The Lord's Prayer.

Prayer Time

Music

The Lord's Prayer

Offering
For all we have received,
and for all we will receive,
Living God,
We give you thanks and praise.
We offer you these gifts
to be light and hope in your world,
for your name's sake, **AMEN**

CAROL - HARK THE HERALD ANGELS SING

Benediction
For all that we have been
For all that we are
And for all that we will be
Living God
We give you thanks and praise.

And may your blessing be upon us
And your hope and joy live in our hearts
Now and always, **AMEN**

The Lord Has Come!

This service has more of a traditional style to it, but there is still space for meditation and reflection. The Advent liturgy is included, if desired, for those who have not had a service in their church on Christmas Day and would like the opportunity to light the central candle on their Advent ring.

The main inspiration for this service was a supermarket advert which used the song "It's beginning to look a lot like Christmas" which posed the question, so what does Christmas look like?

Sensitivity may be needed in the 'Gathering' discussion if there are people in the congregation for whom Christmas has been a difficult time.

The prayer of confession is incorporated into the Prayers of Intercession.

The Lord Has Come

Advent Liturgy

Call to Worship
Great and wonderful are the things
the Lord our God has done for us.
The people who walked in darkness
have seen a great light.   *(Isaiah 9:2)*

The true light that gives light to everyone
has come into the world.
To all who receive him,
he gives power to become children of God.   *(John 1:9)*

CAROL – O LITTLE TOWN OF BETHLEHEM

Gathering – How was Christmas?
How was Christmas for you? Are you overwhelmed with boxes of chocolates, or disappointed at what you did, or didn't get? A vacuum cleaner could fall into either category!

What was your favourite gift?

What was most precious about it?

Prayer of Adoration - Psalm 148 (it may be said antiphonally)

Celebration
Have you noticed that we still talk about celebrating Christmas, even though the word has come to mean something different. It's no longer about giving thanks and being joyful, but more about marking all the traditions associated with the season.

Christmas morning services are a celebration in the former sense, giving thanks and being joyful that Christ is born. We celebrate with the angels who said Christmas about peace and joy.

And we continue to celebrate not only that God bothered with humanity 2000 years ago, but also that God still bothers with us now. We celebrate the promise of new life in every child, and in the Christ-child born to bring salvation to earth.

CAROL – BRIGHTEST AND BEST OF THE SONS OF THE MORNING

Looking like Christmas
Have you ever had an ear-worm? There's no need to look worried, it's not life-threatening or even a medical condition. It's the term people have started to use for an irritating bit of music that goes round and round in your head, and won't go away however hard you try.

The reason for mentioning them is simply that an ear-worm was the inspiration for this morning's reflections. A lot of the adverts leading up to Christmas use well-known Christmas songs, and one in particular recently used "It's beginning to look a lot like Christmas".

Of course, they were trying to sell Christmas decorations and food, so they showed pictures of tinsel, holly wreaths, Christmas lights and beautifully wrapped presents. And then there was the Facebook post from a friend also saying that it was beginning to look a lot like Christmas because she'd been told to "Turn left at the polar bear" when she was being given directions to her room in an hotel!

But what does Christmas really look like? Does it include snow, roaring log fires, polar bears, tinsel and overloaded tables? These are the traditions we are told we need for a perfect Christmas, but they are just trappings, external to the real message of Christmas.

It would be very easy to turn into Ebenezer Scrooge and declare that it is all "humbug", so instead let us think what that first Christmas may have looked like.

An Ordinary Day
It was just an ordinary day,
Except the town was rather busy
Work went on as usual,
People gossiped, worked and moaned,
Just like any other day.

They were milling around,
Ordinary people,
In ordinary clothes,
Doing ordinary things.
Finding lodgings,
Finding food,
Making friends,
Just like any other day.

There were no neon signs
"This way to the God experience"
"This way to eternal salvation".
No preachers shouting warnings
"Tonight your life will change"
There was no one selling tickets
Or tacky souvenirs.
It was just an ordinary day,
Full of ordinary things.

He was just an ordinary man,
Except his inn was rather busy,
who answered those knocks at the door
And they were an ordinary couple,
Dusty, tired and fed-up,
Just like all the rest.

He was an ordinary man,
Who took pity on them,
An ordinary couple,
And gave them some space
In his ordinary stable.

There was no hidden code
Or secret signal
"This will bring you fame and fortune."
"These are extraordinary times."
It was just another day
They were just two more guests.

It was an ordinary night
Except perhaps a little colder,
And the noise from town was louder
With all the visitors there.
And they were ordinary shepherds,
Not specially selected ,
They had not had invitations
To the Almighty Spectacular,
No newspaper ads had brought them there.
"Hear the angels singing,
  Live and Exclusive"
They were ordinary people
Doing an ordinary job.

They saw an ordinary baby,
Five toes on each foot,

Five fingers on each hand,
One head, two arms, two legs.
And all the other delights
Nappies, feeding and wind.
No helpful little halo
Or divine identity card
Because he was an ordinary
In an unusual place,
On an ordinary day.

They were ordinary people
On another ordinary day
Who came to see the baby,
Just another new-born baby,
Just another day.
Without knowing they were seeing,
God become ordinary
In the ordinary way,
In our ordinary world,
On an ordinary day.

CAROL – JESUS IS THE HEART OF CHRISTMAS

Luke 2: 21-38

The Promised Saviour
What did Christmas look like for Simeon and Anna? They had been waiting for many years, patiently, watching everyone who came to the temple day after day. What made them turn to this couple, tired and weary after a long journey, rather than any other? Why turn to a child, a baby?

God had promised them that they would see the salvation of God, but why did they look for it in a child? Wouldn't the obvious people have been the teachers who were in temple courts? But the Holy Spirit guided him to Mary and Joseph, not to someone already established as a teacher, but to a baby, someone yet to make their mark on the world.

And Luke shares with us Simeon's wonderful response –
> 'Master, now you are dismissing your servant in peace,
> according to your word;
> for my eyes have seen your salvation,
> which you have prepared in the presence of all peoples,
> a light for revelation to the Gentiles
> and for glory to your people Israel.'

To Simeon and Anna, Christmas looks like the fulfilment of promises, in unexpected ways. They teach us to look for God in the small and the overlooked, the quiet and the under-valued.

It's not about having the most food, or the largest turkey, but about those with whom it is shared.

It's not about having the most lights on your house, but about letting the light of Christ shine through your life into the lives of others.

Christmas looks like light, shone into the lives of others, for God's sake.

CAROL - WHO WOULD THINK THAT WHAT WAS NEEDED?

Colossians 1: 15-20

This is what Christmas looks like
Paul is very clear about what Christmas looks like: Jesus! In wonderful poetic language he describes Jesus as the image of the invisible God – the one who has come to show us God's plan and intentions, to reveal to us what God is *really* like.

That means if we were still feeling like Scrooge we could have great fun going through the Christmas story and cancelling all the key roles in the nativity plays – there's no mention of a donkey, no innkeeper, no camels, and it probably wasn't in winter.

But that misses the point. It's not about the trappings, it's about how God chose to come to earth. Christmas looks like a small child, born in a stable because there was nowhere else to stay.

So Christmas is not about ostentation, about having the most, or the largest or the best presented. It is about making room at the most difficult time, about setting aside our own concerns and finding time for others.

It is about setting aside our prejudices and values. The first visitors to the stable were the poor and disregarded, the unwanted and unwelcome. So Christmas isn't about what you can get from others, buying only for those who will give to you, it is about recognising the value and humanity of all, and celebrating all that can be offered by everyone.

And it is about looking for God, with Simeon and Anna, not where we most expect to find him, but in unexpected people and unexpected places. We should not be looking in the tinsel and the trappings, but in people, and in promises fulfilled.

For, like Anna and Simeon, and Paul, we know that we have seen the salvation of our God, not in the trappings of Christmas, in wrappings and tinsel, but in the face of our Lord Jesus Christ, who is the image of the invisible God. And God, in Christ, forgives all, and restores all.

And that is the light that Simeon saw, shining from the eyes of a child. May that light shine and guides us through the trappings to the truth of God at the heart of Christmas. AMEN

CAROL – LET EARTH AND HEAVEN COMBINE

Prayers of Intercession
　　"Lord of light, **Shine in our hearts, we pray."**

Eternal God,
the angels sang of "Peace on earth"
and yet we are still at war with one another.
Teach us all how to live together without hatred and jealousy;

Lord of light
Shine in our hearts, we pray.

Faithful God,
Anna and Simeon waited patiently,
but we have become impatient and intolerant,
Teach us all to trust in your promises, and to trust one another.

Lord of light
Shine in our hearts, we pray.

Loving God,
You came to be with the ordinary people
yet we still idolise celebrity and wealth.
Teach us all the true value of love and truth.

Lord of light
Shine in our hearts, we pray.

Healing God,
You came to bring comfort and hope
to those who cried out in need.
Strengthen all those in need today
and surround them with your unending love.

Lord of light
Shine in our hearts, we pray.

We ask these prayers, for your name's sake, **AMEN**

THE LORD'S PRAYER

Offering
Living Lord,
we bring you these gifts
and our lives and our hearts
to be used to show the world
that her Lord has come. **AMEN**

Hymn – Joy to the world, the Lord is come

Benediction
The angels sang:
Glory to God in the highest,
and on earth peace to all in whom he delights.

So as we go into the world God loves so much that he sent his Son for our salvation, let us share the peace and joy of the angels with one another:

The peace of the Lord be always with you.
And also with you.